Britannica Bookshelf-Great Lives

Building the House of Labor
Walter Reuther

Britannica Bookshelf-Great Lives

Building the House of Labor

WALTER REUTHER

by Fred J. Cook

ENCYCLOPAEDIA BRITANNICA PRESS
Chicago   New York   London

Permission to quote from the following works has been granted by the publisher: Louis Ferdinand Celine, Journey to the End of Night, *English translation by John H. P. Marks (Little, Brown & Co., 1934); Keith Sward,* The Legend of Henry Ford *(Holt, Rinehart & Winston, Inc., 1948); Irving Howe and B. J. Widick,* The UAW and Walter Reuther *(Random House, 1949); William Manchester, "Walter Reuther," November, December, 1959.*

TABLE OF CONTENTS

Chapter **1**

The Man

In December of 1962, a short, red-haired, compactly built man hurried into the White House in Washington. With the courtesy shown a distinguished visitor, he was ushered into the President's office. He found the President standing in front of a window, hands clasped behind him, looking out at the White House lawn mantled in snow.

Exhibiting no awe of the Presidential presence, the redhaired visitor quipped lightly: "How does the view of Palm Beach look from there?"

He was referring to the Florida resort city where the President and his family soon were to spend the Christmas holidays. At the jibe, the President turned from the window, the famous grin that had charmed millions lighting his face. "Have you come to support me or advise me?" he asked.

"A bit of both, I hope," his irrepressible visitor told him.

Such was the meeting of John Fitzgerald Kennedy, the third-generation son of Boston Irish immigrants and inheritor of millions, and Walter P. Reuther, the third-generation son of German immigrants born into a hard world beside a West Virginia coal shaft. Kennedy had used money, charm, energy, and the resources of an astute intellect to become President of the United States; Walter Reuther, without money, had used almost the same power—a magnetic personality, a lightning-fast mind, and a drive that left aides exhausted by the wayside—to become one of the most powerful of all the labor leaders of his era. And so they met, these sons of immigrant ancestors, in the office one occupied as President and to which the other had come to speak for the millions of working people he represented.

Despite their banter, both had serious problems on their minds. Walter Reuther, considered by many conservative American businessmen a dangerous radical, had just returned from a tour of Japan, where Communists had rioted in protest against his presence, fearing him as a dangerous salesman of democracy. He had come to the White House straight from three days of labor conferences, disturbing talks concerned with the problems of a lagging American economy and growing joblessness, talks in which special emphasis had been put on the need for expanding opportunities for growth. Around the President even more crucial troubles thronged. In October, he had risked the horror of nuclear war and possible annihilation to drive Soviet missiles out of Cuba; now, the international situation only temporarily stabilized, he was plagued at home by many of the same problems that so concerned Walter Reuther.

Most vexing of all these issues was continuing unemployment. The President had been in office two years, but nearly 5,000,000 workers were still unemployed and the situation

Labor Leaders in the White House; left to right,
then Secretary of Labor Arthur Goldberg;
President of the AFL-CIO George Meany;
President Kennedy; and Walter Reuther

[11]

showed little prospect of improving. The unemployment percentage hovered persistently at almost 6 per cent of the available labor force, and some of the unemployed had been jobless for months, for years. Automation, the rapid supplanting of men by machines, was eliminating jobs at the rate of 2,500,000 a year, and it was doing this just at a time when some 1,200,000 were being added annually to the labor force, largely due to America's outburst of population. The double squeeze exerted by such conflicting pressures obviously was creating a looming crisis. But the nation as a whole seemed unaware—and uncaring. Most of the people were relatively prosperous, and so there was no public outcry for action, no pressure on Congress. The President had been trying to make Congress and the nation see the dangers of persistent unemployment, coupled with the steady wiping out of jobs by automation; he had been stressing the necessity for tax cuts and reforms to spur the economy and create more jobs. But his words had been treated almost with indifference, and Congress seemed certain to follow the path of least resistance and do little or nothing.

"How do you make people understand the seriousness of this problem, of the meaning of that 6 per cent unemployed?" the President asked in exasperation.

Ask Walter Reuther almost any question, and you get a fast answer. There is, it seems at times, almost no social or economic problem of any significance that he has not studied and deeply pondered. And so he had a fast answer ready now.

"Well, you can't get anywhere by discussing the problem in terms of percentages, Mr. President," he responded. "If you pose the issue in that framework, that there are 6 per cent unemployed, you are licked; you are playing your opponent's game. Your opposition says instantly, 'But 94 per cent *are* employed,' and you can't get anywhere discussing it in those terms. Ninety-four per cent is going to beat 6 per cent any day. There is only one thing you can do. You must argue the case in terms of people."

Recalling that conversation the following day in his office in the United Automobile Workers' huge headquarters, Solidarity House in Detroit, Walter Reuther leaned forward eagerly at his desk, grabbed paper and pencil, and illustrated exactly what he had meant when he told President Kennedy that unemployment statistics must be discussed, not in terms of percentages, but in terms of people.

"Take Chicago, for example," he said. "They've made substantial progress in reducing unemployment. They've cut it back to less than 3 per cent. But—and this is the significant fact—some 22 per cent of the Negroes are unemployed."

Capping this illustration with another, Reuther quoted the latest monthly unemployment figures. These showed that another 500,000 persons had been thrown out of work, but the important fact to Reuther was that some 150,000 of these were youths futilely seeking their first jobs. Of the nearly 5,000,000 unemployed well over 1,000,000 were youths, ranging from 16 into their early 20's who were both out of work and out of school, and thus left with no place to go but on the streets.

"When you put that 6 per cent unemployed in terms of the people involved, it isn't just a meaningless 6 per cent," he argued. "When you put it in terms of people—the Negroes, youths seeking their first jobs and unable to get a start in life—you can see the enormous group pressures that are being built up, the tragic wastes in human resources, the tremendous potentialities for trouble.

"When a man is unemployed, it doesn't mean anything to him that he's just part of a mere 6 per cent. His hunger, his need, his frustration are his, and they are acute, and they are the only things that matter."

Tipping back in his desk chair, his eyes alight, his ruddy face with its pixie smile vibrant, he summed up the advice he had given the President.

"I told him that the only thing that has value is people," he said. "And you know it's true. Not money, not power. There are no values unrelated to people."

In that sentence is distilled the essence of Walter Reuther. He considers himself, he says, "a pragmatic idealist." In him, this merger of the practical and the visionary has been a happy marriage. The practical part of his nature has brought him far, all the way from the desolate West Virginia hills, all the way from humble status as a tool and die maker in Detroit's auto factories, up to the pinnacle of union power and national prominence, so that today he speaks on equal terms with heads of state. It is the kind of climb that has made many men callous. But not Reuther. He becomes almost lyrical about people.

"People are wonderful," he says. "They have all kinds of untapped possibilities and resources; there is absolutely no limit to what they can do if you can only communicate with them and unlock those hidden powers. People have never let me down. There have been times in my life when I have been in seemingly impossible situations, when the odds against me were so fantastic it seemed impossible I could ever win. But at those times I placed my faith in

[14]

people. I felt that if I could only communicate the truth to them, if I could only make them understand the facts, they would never let me down—and they never have."

The words do not come glibly from Reuther. He is no sentimental theorist, philosophizing without abrasive contact with the rough edges of life. Few men, indeed, have seen more of life's seamy side or been subjected to rougher buffeting. His experiences would have been enough to daunt the average, more sheltered man. For Walter Reuther is a man who has known firsthand the brutal clutch of poverty; he was reared in impoverished surroundings and had to quit school and go to work at 16. He is a man who has seen with his own eyes the incredible brutalities of the Hitler, Mussolini, and Stalin dictatorships. He is a man who, in the union wars of the 1930's, was brutally beaten by company goons. He is a man who was almost killed, his right arm nearly severed from his body, by a shotgun blast from the weapon of a hired assassin. He is a man who saw his closest brother, Victor, almost killed in a similar, murderous attempt. He is a man who, since these crimes were never solved, still lives in the shadow of murder—a man who still has to keep guards around his home, who is accompanied by a bodyguard wherever he goes. And yet he remains a man who, having seen and tasted the depths of human evil, refuses to be shaken in the faith he utters with a passionate sincerity:

"Only people are important. The only thing that counts is people."

Chapter 2

The Boy

Walter Philip Reuther was born in Wheeling, West Virginia, on September 1, 1907, a date most aptly timed. It was Labor Day eve.

"I got off to a fast start in life," Reuther says, with a grin. "I think I chose my mother and father and my grandparents with great care."

In later life, many powerful men were to be baffled by the spectacle of Walter Reuther, a man who seemed to operate by rules quite different from the rules of their club. Perhaps they would not have been so astonished had they appreciated the strong family tradition that still influences his life today. For the guidelines that he came to adopt were not strange; for him, they were natural.

The social consciousness that is such a strong Reuther family trait stems back to Walter's grandfather, Jacob Reuther, a devout if unorthodox Lutheran and a passionate, bearded Social Democrat. In 1892, Jacob gave up his German farm and emigrated to the United States because he did not wish to see his children subjected to Prussian military service. In the new country, he remained very much his same sturdy, independent self. He continued to agitate for the improvement of social conditions, and he became quite an amateur theologian, writing a number of treatises critical of official Lutheran Church policy. His principal contention was that the church emphasisized the hereafter too much and the here-and-now not enough. He did not quarrel with the premise that a heavenly reward awaited the virtuous, but he argued that more persons would be virtuous if crushing economic and social conditions were relieved. And he thought that the Church should not abstain, as it then did, from involvement in earthly problems, but rather should take the lead in trying to solve them.

This strong strand of social philosophy was passed on by Jacob Reuther to his son, Valentine, and even to his grandsons who, in later years, were to read some of his theological arguments and be much impressed by them. In the Reuther family, it was almost as if one generation handed the brand to the next, and the new torchbearers raced off full tilt, carrying the light. One of the strongest of all the runners in this three-generation marathon was Jacob's son, Valentine.

Valentine early became a fiery unionist and a leader of the Brewery Workers. He had the good fortune to marry red-haired Anna Stoker, a girl whose spunk matched his own, and they went to live in Wheeling, where Valentine earned the princely salary of $1.50 a day working at the Schmulbach Brewery. His job was to drive a brewery wagon over mountain roads in all kinds of weather, in rain and snow and sub-zero temperatures. His route took him clear to the Pennsylvania border, and he was sometimes on the road 17 hours at a stretch. Walter Reuther still recalls how his father, after such a long ordeal, sometimes would be so stiffened with cold that he would have to be lifted from the wagon and thawed out before he could walk. It was a rugged life, but Anna and Valentine Reuther were a rugged couple.

"My mother and father," Walter Reuther says, "were simply wonderful human beings. We had all the economic difficulties, all the problems that many American families had in those days, but mother and father raised the family around a simple basic philosophy. My father always tried to make us understand that our lives were going to be successes or failures, not according to material values, whether we were rich or poor, but whether we had really made a contribution to making the world a better place to live in."

No matter how hard life was in the Reuther family—and there were times when it was cruelly, unbelievably hard—Anna and Valentine Reuther tried to impress upon their children by their conduct the code with which they governed their own lives. For a time Anna was in poor health, and the boys had to learn to cook and do the household chores. It was even worse when Valentine went temporarily blind and could not work. He lost the sight of one eye, and for a time the sight of the other was impaired.

"Mother had four young kids to support," Walter recalls, "but no matter how hard things were, she never complained, she never lost faith. No matter how little we had to eat, mother and father always took in every tramp that came along and sat them down at our table. Dad would always say to us: 'I want you to remember that, as long as you have something to eat, you have to share it with others who haven't.' It was his way, I guess, of teaching us applied Christianity."

Even such family hardships could not cool the ardor of Valentine Reuther. He became the youngest president the Ohio Valley Trades and Labor Assembly had ever had. A young man in his 30's, he ran for Congress on the Socialist ticket. Like his father, he became indignant at the casual attitude of the Lutheran Church toward worldly problems; and when the local pastor held that the welfare of man was no concern of God, Valentine indignantly quit the Church and organized Sunday debates in his own family circle on social problems of the day. Walter still vividly remembers those debates. Everyone in the family, he recalls, was encouraged to speak up, to take a position and then battle his strongest for it. This boyhood practice became a way of life. Walter has been speaking up—and battling—ever since.

The Reuther home at 3640 Wetzel Street in South Wheeling was a frame rectangle house with three rooms downstairs and three up. Valentine Reuther had built it with his own hands. It had no halls, no artistic arrangement of rooms. One simply stepped through the front door into the living room, from the living room into the dining room, from the dining room into the kitchen. Beyond the kitchen was the dwelling's one novelty. In those days an outhouse squatted at a distance behind nearly every home, but Valentine, with an eye to modern plumbing, had constructed a little bathroom on a covered porch tacked on behind the kitchen. The only trouble was that one had to duck outdoors in the cold and approach it across the porch.

Originally, when the family was small, just the downstairs rooms were used in winter, all meals were eaten in the kitchen, and the dining room was turned into a bedroom. Later, as the family grew, the upstairs rooms were put to use. There were four boys, born almost exactly two years apart, and much later, a girl, Christine. Theodore, the oldest, was born in 1905; next came Walter. Roy was two years younger than him, and Victor two years younger than Roy.

The Reuther home was located almost in the heart of a mining and industrial area. Two blocks away was the brewery where Valentine Reuther reported for work at 4 A.M. Right next door was the entrance to an abandoned coal mine, and Walter still recalls how, as a boy, he accompanied his father into the mine and helped to pull locust posts out of the shaft to use them as fence posts. Close by was a paper mill, and not much farther off, a glass factory, which especially fascinated Walter. "They had almost no safety rules in those days," he recalls, "and I remember how, as a small boy, I used to walk through the glass factory on stilts."

To the boy on stilts the glass factory had about it an almost fairyland quality. The workers were real artists, and it was fascinating to watch them as they fashioned lovely and unusual designs in molten glass. Punch bowls laced with intricate figures and lampshades decorated with flowers, or graced with the attractive forms of strolling women, materialized like magic before the eyes of the watching boy. He soon became familiar with the pattern of the work and the factory routine. First, skilled metal workers, real artists in their own right, would create in a steel mold the design that was to be reproduced in glass; the mold would then go to the glassblowers who would take molten glass, bubbling from the furnace, and begin to blow it into the mold. This glassblowing was a complicated process. The liquid glass had to

[21]

be blown into the mold with precision; it had to be turned just right and cooled just gradually enough so that it would not crack. There were six stages to this process, six separate stations along the glassblowing line, and so there developed a need for what were called "carry boys." The cooling glass would be placed upon a large asbestos paddle, and the "carry boys" took it from one craftsman to another.

"When they needed an extra boy, they would hire a 12-year-old, anybody who happened to be available," Walter recalls. "I hung around that glass factory a great deal, and I remember especially I hung around the place where they made the punch bowls. One was a beautiful thing. I still remember it. The glass was a beautiful crimson color, and it had woven into it a design in gold. The gold had to be added at just the right time, and it was quite a ceremony in the plant when the glass was ready for the gold. Then the president of the company would come by with five or six gold pieces, and he would throw these in to be melted and fused into the glass, reproducing the design."

Fascinated by such wonders, Walter practically lived in the glass factory, and by the time he was 10 or 11, he had become almost a fixture in the department where the skilled steelworkers made the molds. Young as he was, he sensed that this was the heart of the entire enterprise; these were the men who really created the designs the glass workers would reproduce; and he wanted to get as close as he could to this center of creativity. So he hung about the workbenches until finally the workers gave him a piece of steel and a hammer and chisel, and let him sit beside them, trying to hammer out his own ideas on metal, while they worked creating molds.

[22]

"This was why I later became a tool and die maker," Walter says. "I was fascinated by the skill of these men in creating molds that made the most beautiful things. Some of them tried to show me how to work the steel and make designs in it, and for a time my highest ambition was to work in the glass factory. But the men themselves warned me against it. Technology was already putting them out of business. Machines could stamp out designs much faster and cheaper, and it was becoming obvious that soon there would be no place for the hand craftsman. In fact, it wasn't too long before the glass factory had to go out of business." It was Walter Reuther's first experience with the problem of technology, with that battle of man and machine that was to preoccupy so much of his later life.

At the time, Walter was more concerned with ways to help out the straitened family finances. "Hard work was considered a virtue in our family," he recalls. "We all had chores, tending the garden, taking care of rabbits and chickens and guinea pigs." The vegetables and chickens helped to fill out the family larder, but it was still a struggle to make ends meet—just how much of a struggle is perhaps best illustrated by the story of Anna Reuther's black umbrella.

Anna had wanted a good umbrella in the worst way and had scraped and saved pennies until she was able to buy one. The black cloth gleamed, and the new umbrella was the pride of her life. Unfortunately, the shiny new item caught the speculative eye of one of her young sons, and being a boy, he began to figure. What was the use of worrying about the rain? Wouldn't that umbrella be put to better use as a parachute? The thought led to prompt and disastrous experiment. At the first jump, the ribs of the umbrella all whipped up and the fabric tore apart. Anna Reuther's new prize was a wreck, but in the Reuther household it was not a wreck to be discarded. Recovering from her exasperation, Anna set out to salvage what she could, and from the torn black cloth, she made a shirt for one of the boys.

When even a ripped umbrella becomes an item of value, one gets some idea of the pressures on the Reuther household. To help out, all of the boys, as soon as they were old enough, worked at odd jobs, earning whatever they could after school and on weekends. The oldest brother, Ted, finished grade school, took a year's course in business school, and by the time he was 16 was a full-time wage earner. Walter, also trying to help, got a job delivering newspapers every morning.

"I carried the Wheeling *Register* for a number of years," he recalls. "I would leave home at four o'clock in the morning and go over to the same barn my father had driven the brewery wagons from. The American Express Company ran the barn, and they had wagons going down to the Wheeling depot. There was one certain driver who was a friend of mine, and I would get a ride with him at 4:30 every morning. This would get me into Wheeling about 5:15, and I would get my papers.

"I have always been able, wherever I went, to make friends with people, and it wasn't long before I was friendly with the circulation foreman. He would always give me a few extra papers, sometimes as many as 50. This was quite a windfall for me, but I never sold them. I just gave them away to my friends. All along my route, I had friends, and when I got extra copies, I saw to it that they got free copies.

[24]

Those I had left when I finished my route, I always gave to a blind man who ran a newsstand at 12th and Market Streets.

"My route covered the business area. To carry my papers, I had a little wagon that I had made myself. It was painted blue, with red letters on it. When I was finished, I always kept three papers to dispose of on the way home. Every morning, I caught one special trolley. It was much like the Toonerville Trolley in the comic papers. The motorman and conductor were friends of mine, and I would give them each a paper and they would put my wagon on the trolley and let me ride home free.

"The third paper I always kept for a family that were good friends of ours. They lived just below 35th Street in South Wheeling, and every morning as we passed their house, I would fold up the paper and sail it, trying to hit the porch. I became pretty expert at it, and usually I landed the paper right on the porch. In time, it became quite a game; and the motorman, just to make it a little more difficult for me, would sometimes speed up the trolley just as we were passing the house. One morning he either speeded up more than I had anticipated, or I miscalculated, for when I threw the folded paper, it sailed right through the big plate glass window overlooking the porch. I'm afraid my friends could have bought a lot of papers for what that window cost."

Having finished delivering his papers, Walter would return home, get a hasty breakfast, and go off to school. He excelled at manual training, as it was then called—at all kinds of shop and mechanical work. "I still have in my home a beat-up copper ashtray that I made in grade school," Walter recalls. "It is not an accomplished work of art, but I still think it's pretty good." In his sophomore year in high

[25]

school, his skill in the machine shop was such that he became an assistant to his teacher.

Besides shop, Walter's great enthusiasm was athletics. He and his younger brother, Roy, were both star basketball players. Roy was an inch taller than Walter, who stands about 5 feet 8 inches, but Walter had so much more bounce than Roy, or anyone else, that invariably he was chosen to play center. In summer, the Reuther boys switched from basketball to baseball, and Walter pitched and played shortstop. One year their YMCA team won the tri-state junior championship, and an old family photograph shows Walter and Roy, chests proudly stuck out, posing behind a chair on which stands their mother's bread board, festooned with the ribbons and medals they had won in athletic contests.

Such was Walter Reuther's life until he was 16. In the Reuther family, 16 was the age when a man went to work, and Walter was no exception. All during his last year in high school, when he was 15, he was taking on extra work, sampling other jobs, his eye on the future. While he was still in school, he got one job working in a bakery from 7 o'clock Friday nights until 8:30 Saturday morning. This meant that he could not deliver his papers on Saturdays, and he had to hire a friend to handle the paper route for him. But the bakery, he thought, might open the way to permanent employment. And it doubtless would have, for the baker liked Walter and wanted to hire him as a full time apprentice. "I had decided by that time, however," Walter says, with a wry grin, "that the bakery wasn't for me. At four o'clock every Saturday morning, I had to clean up the dough mixer after the dough had dried. Did you ever try to clean a dough mixer?" He shakes his head. "That was

Walter and Roy Reuther and their sports trophies

[27]

enough to discourage me from ever becoming a journeyman baker."

In the summer when he was 15, still searching, he got a job with the Wheeling Corrugating Company, making inside liners for the glass doors of ovens that sat on top of gas stoves. "It was piecework," Walter says, "and I worked my tail off, but I made more money than anybody else on the job." Such piecework, however, obviously offered no future to a young man starting out in life; and so the next year, when Walter quit school at 16, he hired himself out as an apprentice in the machine shop of Wheeling Steel. Though he didn't know it at the time, he had set his foot on the long road that was to lead to the auto factories of Detroit and his life's career as a union leader.

Chapter *3*

Start of the Trail

Walter Reuther worked three years in Wheeling Steel. It was an invaluable experience, for he had an opportunity to learn more things faster than he ever would have in a larger and more specialized shop. Characteristically, Walter took advantage of every opportunity.

He began, as all apprentices begin, doing the dirtiest jobs in the place. One of these involved oiling the pulleys of the operating machinery. In the process, the oiler always became spattered and drenched with oil and grease. "When you finished, you looked as if you had just come out of a coal mine," Walter says.

After a year of such grimy labor, Walter was promoted and shifted to the new tool and die department. Tool and die makers are among the elite workers of industry. Huge dies, made out of specially hardened metal with sharp cutting edges, are used to stamp out in softer metal the gears and parts of other pieces of machinery, and so the men who design and fashion and handle the dies are key workers.

[29]

"I learned to do everything," he says today. "For example, they would bring us a beat-up piece of metal and say, 'We've got to make this.' We would have to make all the drawings, design the part, make the dies, and finally fashion the piece of machinery that had to be replaced."

While Walter was learning the trade of a tool and die maker, he was also demonstrating the stern stuff of which he was made. In his second year at Wheeling Steel, he experienced the first of the lifelong series of tragic injuries that was to leave his body as scarred as any soldier's. The accident tells much about his drive and determination.

One day a rush order came through to move a heavy die from a press. The die was a huge piece of metal, weighing about 400 pounds. The orders were to get it out of the press —and get it out fast.

"It was one of those cases where we were being pressed, we were being rushed to work too fast, and we didn't take time to think or take proper safety precautions," Reuther explains. Three men and himself, gripping the die with their hands, tried to hoist it out of the press.

"It had oil on the underside," Walter remembers. "When we got it almost out, our hands started to slip in the oil, and we knew that we were going to lose control of it." In such circumstances, what could a 17-year-old boy be expected to do? Most probably would have dropped the die and jumped back out of the road of the plunging juggernaut. But not Walter Reuther.

"The only thing I could think of," he recalls, "is that, if I let go, perhaps one of my fellow workers would be killed. Even then, I think, probably as the result of my training at home, I had this tremendous concern for my fellow man, this feeling that he was my responsibility, and I was afraid that if I let go, the die might crash down on one of the others."

So Walter clung doggedly to his side of the slipping die, and when it crashed, it crashed in his direction. The sharp edge of the die, with all the shearing power of 400 plunging pounds behind it, came crashing down on the concrete floor. It sliced through the leather shoe of Walter's right foot as if it had been paper, sliced off his right big toe. "Even so, I was lucky," Walter says. "If the die had crashed a few inches further back, it would have taken off my whole foot."

At the moment, of course, Walter could not count such blessings. With blood spurting from his foot, he was placed on a stretcher, carried to an ambulance, and rushed to the hospital. Before he left, however, he made one strange request. He shouted to his fellow workers: "Bring me that toe! I'm not going to the hospital without my toe."

Mystified but impelled by Walter's frantic insistence, the workers rescued the toe, placed it on the stretcher with Walter; and toe and Walter rode to the hospital. "All I could think of," Walter explains today, "was that this meant the end of my basketball career. I was always the shortest guy on the team, but I always jumped center because I could jump so much higher than anybody else. Now I could see that I wasn't going to be able to jump so high unless I had two big toes."

This secret worry led, once Walter had reached the hospital, to one of the strangest scenes ever enacted between a doctor and his patient. "I'm sorry," the doctor told Walter, "but there is nothing I can do about your toe. I'll have to just sew up the wound, but don't worry. You'll be all right." The doctor, who could not appreciate what two big toes could mean to a fellow, had reckoned without his patient.

"You'll do nothing of the kind," Walter cried. "I want that toe sewed back on."

"But's that's crazy," the doctor protested. "I can't save your toe. It's been completely severed—bone, blood vessels, everything. There's no way I can sew it on."

"You don't know how important this is," Walter raged. "You don't know how important it is to me to have two big toes! I won't let you touch me unless you agree to sew that toe on."

The argument raged on, but the doctor soon found, as other adversaries were to find later, that there was no use arguing with Walter when his mind was made up. "All right," the doctor finally conceded, "it's the craziest thing I ever heard of, but I'll do it. We'll give you an anesthetic, and I'll sew the toe on."

"Oh, no, you won't," Walter told him. "You won't give me any anesthetic. I want to see what you're doing."

He explains today that he feared he might be tricked— that he thought, once the doctor had him under anesthesia, he might just sew up the wound. Walter was determined that he wasn't going to be deprived of his big toe in such fashion; and the dismayed doctor, finally beaten down by his patient's insistence, was compelled to agree.

"It took three guys to hold me down while he did it," Walter remembers. "And, of course, the doctor had been right all the time; it was all for nothing. In a few days, they had to take me back to the hospital and amputate.

"I hadn't been able to save the toe, but I was determined that I wouldn't be a cripple, that I would never walk with a limp. That's harder than you might think. Unconsciously, you have a tendency to compensate, to take the pressure off and lean a bit to one side. But I forced myself to walk upright, no matter how much it hurt, and I determined that, toe or no toe, I was going to play basketball again. Of course, it slowed me down a bit for a time, but in the end I did play basketball. When I was at Ford, I organized the Highland Park basketball team, and I jumped center, and we won a championship."

Even today, nearly 40 years later, Walter Reuther is reminded of that old accident every time he buys a new pair of shoes. "The pain is excruciating every step I take until I get them broken in," he says. But he refuses now, just as he did then, to make any concession to pain; he carries himself erectly as any soldier.

This kind of determination, obviously, was a quality too big to be contained by a city the size of Wheeling. Walter confesses frankly that it wasn't the lack of economic opportunity in Wheeling that motivated his move (after all, he had been accustomed all his life to do with very little); but he realized: "If I was to reach out, I would have to have more elbow room." Instinctively, he knew that he must seek opportunity in a larger field; and so at 19, having worked three years at Wheeling Steel, he decided to go to Detroit and seek employment in the automobile factories.

No young man ever made so daring a decision at a worse time. The date was February of 1927. The Ford Motor Company had decided to drop the Model T, the car that had made it famous, the car that, for the first time, had brought an automobile within the reach of every American family. Ford was replacing the Model T with the Model A, a task

[33]

that required the complete retooling of its factories. And while Ford was retooling, its assembly lines were closed down. As a result Detroit was a stricken city. Thousands of unemployed workers roamed the streets and queued up in long lines, competing for the few jobs that were available.

Walter knew before he left Wheeling that the prospects in Detroit were far from bright. One of the girls in a neighboring family had married a worker in Detroit, and, hearing of Walter's contemplated move, she wrote a frank description of conditions there, trying to discourage him. But, says Walter, in what must be the understatement of many a year, "I was a very hard kid to discourage. I came anyhow."

With the help of the former neighbor, Walter found a room with a Southern family and set out to look for work. He had anticipated that job hunting would be very rough indeed, but he had never realized it was going to be *this* rough. "I stood at five o'clock in the morning in zero weather in long lines of workers applying for jobs," Walter recalls. Day after day he chased a job, and finally he landed one at the Briggs Manufacturing Company plant. Briggs, then independently owned, had a reputation among workers in those pre-union days as the worst plant in Detroit in which to work, and this may explain how Walter Reuther, with his baby-pink complexion, looking as he says "like I fell off a green-apple tree," managed to get a job when so many more experienced Detroiters were unemployed. Certainly, the job was a backbreaker—a 13-hour night shift doing big, heavy die work. But to Walter it represented opportunity; it assured him of a foothold in Detroit—and that was what he was seeking.

"I worked 13 hours a night 21 straight nights at Briggs," Walter says, and he indicates that, by the end of that time, the Briggs job was getting too much even for him. But as usual he was not without resources; as usual, he had made friends. A foreman who had taken a liking to him suggested that he apply at Burroughs, makers of adding machines and office equipment, where they were reported to be hiring men. The report was wrong. Burroughs wasn't hiring anybody; but the hiring boss, perhaps trying to be helpful, perhaps just having some sport with Walter, said that he had heard Ford, in its development of the Model A, was now hiring die leaders. These were key men, expert diemakers with some 25 years experience and so qualified to supervise the activities of squads of five or six skilled workers.

"I went home and slept on it," Walter says. "I was 19, but I looked like 16, with my red cheeks, red hair, and the complexion of a 13-year-old girl." This critical self-appraisal might have deterred almost anyone but Walter Reuther from applying for a job that required 25 years' experience. But Walter was never one to be awed by obstacles. He looked up bus schedules; and the next day, after spending the night working at Briggs, he hurried to his rooming house, washed, dressed, and boarded a bus that would take him out to Ford's huge Highland Park plant. When the bus stopped and let him off, Walter stood for a moment and stared in wonder and fascination. "I had never seen anything that big before."

Gathering his courage, he advanced upon the employment entrance, and there, at the door, he found a "great, big, burly" guard. "Good morning," Walter said to the stern looking man politely. "I understand you're hiring die leaders."

"Yes," growled the guard.

"Well, that's what I am," Walter told him blandly.

[35]

The guard took a close look at Walter and reacted angrily at this insult to his intelligence. "Come on, get out of here," he roared. "You're nothing but a kid."

Walter refused to budge. "Are you a die leader?"

"You know I'm not or I wouldn't be here."

"Well," said Walter, "you must be an extremely valuable man to your organization. Any man who can tell just by looking at somebody whether he's a die leader or not must be a mighty important man."

Evidently, nobody had ever subjected the guard to this kind of a flank attack before; and the poor, befuddled master of brawn couldn't quite make up his mind whether he was being taunted, insulted, or complimented. So he made the mistake of arguing with Walter. The verbal duel lasted two and a half hours. When he ended, Walter was just as fresh and argumentative as when he started, but the guard was exasperated and exhausted.

"All right," he said finally, "I give up. I'll call the hiring manager. They'll probably fire me, but it's the only way I know of getting rid of you." The hiring manager came, took one look at Walter, and reacted exactly as the guard had.

"Are you, sir, a die leader?" Walter asked politely.

"You know I'm not," said the hiring manager.

Around and around they went. Finally, Walter said, "Look, there's one thing a young man can do nothing about —and that's his age. I can't do anything about the fact that I'm 19, but I don't see how you can look at me and say I'm not a die leader."

He kept insisting that he would not leave until he had met someone who could judge his talents fairly. His persistence finally wore down the hiring manager, just as it had the guard; and so Walter was passed along to the foreman in charge of the die department—a tall, thin man who looked much like Henry Ford himself. As soon as he saw Walter, he reacted just as the others had, and the argument began all over again. As it happened, the foreman was carrying a roll of blueprints under his arm, and Walter, pointing to these, finally issued a challenge. "Look," he said, "you have blueprints there. Let's roll them out and see how much I know or don't know. If you say, 'No,' after that, I'll leave very quietly."

Since leaving very quietly was all that everybody wanted Walter to do, the foreman accepted the challenge and spread out the blueprints. Walter, to the foreman's surprise, promptly demonstrated that he could read a blueprint as well as the next man; and, once he had passed this test, he promptly pressed his advantage. "All right," he said, "now I have proved to you that I can read a blueprint. But you'll never know how much else I can do unless you hire me. Hire me and find out."

The foreman, of course, realized that Walter could not possibly be a die leader, but this brash, confident young man might very well be an excellent diemaker. At least, nothing yet had disproved his claims, and it was obvious that, having passed the blueprint test, he no longer had any intention of departing "very quietly." "I tell you what I'll do," the foreman said. "If you'll agree to work here two days without knowing how much you'll be paid, we'll watch you and then we'll decide. That's my offer. Take it or leave it."

"I'll take it," Walter said.

He left the plant and rushed back to Briggs. Sleep now became important to him. He had worked 13 hours the previous night; he had spent the entire day arguing at Ford; and he had to report for work at the Ford gate in the morning. He wanted to collect his tools at Briggs, go home, and rest up. But to do this, he needed a clearance from the night supervisor to take his tools out of the Briggs plant. And the night supervisor, a stubborn man, refused to give him such a clearance.

Walter had been making 75 cents an hour. The supervisor, not wanting to lose him, offered him 80 cents to stay at Briggs. Walter refused. He had a chance for a job with Ford and he intended to make the most of it. Another argument started. It lasted all night. "That S.O.B. kept me there until 6 A.M. before he would give me a tool clearance," Walter recalls. "I had to get a taxi to get out to the Ford plant in time to report for work."

There, bone weary from two sleepless nights and a sleepless day, Walter worked a regular eight-hour shift, conscious that the critical eyes of plant supervisors were watching every move he made. Those hours, he confesses, were the longest and the hardest he ever worked. But somehow he survived them, and the next day, at the end of his second trick, the foreman and another boss came over to him. "Well, young man," the foreman said, "you have certainly surprised all of us. We've watched you, and you haven't done anything wrong yet. The job is yours at $1.05 an hour."

Only a few weeks before, Walter had been making a mere 42 cents an hour at Wheeling Steel. Now he had more than doubled his salary. And he had done it at the worst possible time, under the worst possible circumstances. No doubt about it, the determined young redhead from Wheeling was on his way.

[38]

Chapter *4*

He Grows and Learns

Detroit was an education for Walter Reuther—in more ways than one. In the teeming life of the Motor City, he became aware for the first time of problems whose dimensions he had not even glimpsed in the quieter atmosphere of Wheeling. One of the most important of these was the racial issue. "I had to come to Detroit to know there even was such a thing," Walter explains. "I had heard about it before, of course, but in our family there just wasn't any such thing, or even a thought of it. To me, the whole business wasn't real, and it wasn't until I came to Detroit that I really experienced it, really realized what it was."

Detroit may seem like a strange place for a youth from Wheeling, West Virginia, to bump hard for the first time into the problem of discrimination, but actually it was a logical place. The city was a hotbed of racial tensions—such a hotbed that, not too many years later, it was to be shaken by one of the bloodiest race riots ever to take place in America. The background for the growth of the racial issue in Detroit lies in the development of the automobile industry.

Henry Ford, one of the greatest and most ruthless production geniuses in United States history, had perfected the assembly line. Automobile manufacturing was broken down into thousands of simple operations. Parts moved on conveyor belts, and each worker inserted his screw or tightened his nut, an action he repeated endlessly throughout each long working shift. In this new system, no man actually built or created anything; no skilled labor was needed. Raw farm hands could be quickly trained to perform the quick, mechanical actions that were all the assembly line demanded of them. The labor itself was boring, stultifying drudgery, and the men who performed it became mere automatons, dehumanized arms and legs, who kept constantly feeding the ever moving, ever demanding line.

The process turned men into virtual zombies. Frequently, unable to stand the deadly monotony, rebelling at the subhuman status that the machines they tended had reduced them to, workers threw up their jobs in disgust and went off on a binge or desperately sought some other way of making a livelihood. But, eventually, they came back, most of them, to the only kind of work they knew. Under the circumstances, the labor turnover in the automobile plants was terrific; it was a constant management headache. Then, in 1914, Henry Ford announced he would pay $5 a day.

Five dollars a day in an age when many workers were trying to raise families on salaries of $10 to $15 a week seemed like a fortune. There were many catches to Ford's offer and the $5 a day was not the great philanthropy it seemed; but the catches, the brutal conditions in the auto factories, weren't apparent until the worker was already hooked, already chained to the assembly line. The result was that the lure of Ford's $5 a day brought a mass of unskilled labor streaming into Detroit. Hillbillies trekked down from the Tennessee and Kentucky mountains, and from all over the South came a great migration of Negroes. It was a dangerous, explosive mixture.

Many of the Southerners who came to the great Michigan city brought with them racial prejudices ingrained in the bone for generations. Typical was the attitude of the Southern family with whom Walter Reuther first roomed in Detroit. "They were wonderful people, and they were very good to me," Walter says. "But they were true Southerners, and they had certain prejudices, and these were very pronounced."

The Southerners made no secret of their detestation of the Negroes, yet they were a very religious family, all ardent Baptists, and they were anxious to have Walter attend church with them. Walter kept putting them off. It was not that he was irreligious. As a boy, he had walked three miles to the Lutheran Sunday School every Sunday, and he had gone for seven years without missing a class. As a Lutheran, he harbored no prejudice against the Baptists. What disturbed him was the seeming lack of any connection between the principles of religion and the race prejudice of the family.

"I don't see why you won't go to church with us," one of the men of the family said one day to Walter.

"Well, I would like to go with you," Walter told him, "but I am a little disturbed. I don't see how you equate your religion with what you do all the other days of the week toward your brother who is black."

[41]

The Southerners couldn't understand this attitude, and they kept pressing Walter to attend church with them. Finally, Walter decided to offer them a sporting proposition.

"All right," he said one day, "I'll go to church with you this coming Sunday provided you can answer one question to my satisfaction. Will you do that?"

"Certainly," the Southerner agreed.

"I know you," Walter said. "I know you're a good Christian; I know that you believe in Christian values and that a man who lives his life by them will be rewarded and go to Heaven. Isn't that so?"

The Southerner acknowledged that Walter was right.

"All right," said Walter, "now for my question: Do you believe that a Negro who lives his life according to the Scripture, who adheres to the same Christian values that you do, will also be rewarded and go to the same Heaven?"

"No. Of course not!" the Southerner exclaimed.

"Well, you see," said Walter, with his must cherubic smile, "that's why I cannot go to church with you."

This finally settled the matter, but it did not end—indeed, it was only the beginning—of Walter Reuther's long preoccupation with the problem of racial discrimination.

It did not take Walter long to establish himself solidly in Detroit. He soon became recognized as one of the most skilful diemakers in Ford's Highland Park plant, and he worked on the most delicate jobs, calling for the highest precision. The young redhead impressed many men, none more so than the tall, lean foreman whose roll of blueprints Walter had read so easily in his first qualifying test.

The foreman became very friendly, invited Walter to his home for dinner, and introduced him to his wife. After

Walter had visited them several times, the foreman drew him aside and said he wanted to talk to him privately. He explained that he and his wife had never been able to have any children of their own and that they had both become greatly attached to Walter. "My wife and I think you should come to live with us," the foreman said. "It would be to us like having a son of our own. It would complete our home for us."

Walter was astonished by the offer, and when he reminisces about it today, he still seems deeply touched. The decision he had to make was one of the most difficult he ever faced, for he felt that he had to refuse yet he did not wish to hurt the couple, who meant him the greatest kindness.

"I was afraid," he explained, "that it would change my relationship with my boss in the factory. I was afraid I would be getting something I wasn't earning, or even if I wasn't, that fellow workers in the factory might think that I was. I didn't want favors I wasn't entitled to, and I felt the whole situation would be an awkward one, both for him and for me."

Walter explained all this as gently and carefully as he could, and the foreman and his wife, though disappointed, understood and respected his decision.

All this time, Walter was helping his parents and his family back in West Virginia. "The first pay check I got," he says, "I figured out how much I needed for the week, and I sent the rest home to my parents. I didn't have to do it; nobody asked me to, or expected me to. It was just one of those things that it seemed natural to me to do, and I did it without thinking about it. My father wrote back and said that they appreciated the check, but it wasn't necessary for me to send it. I ignored him and kept right on sending the checks. Each week, after I had set aside what I had to have for my own needs, I would send them the rest. Finally, right after my 21st birthday, my father returned the last check to me and wrote: 'I won't take any more money from you.' " It was Valentine Reuther's way of saying that Walter was a man now and, as a man, he would need his own money.

Walter's success as a tool and die maker soon lured his brothers Roy and Victor to follow him to Detroit. The three brothers rented an apartment. Roy, a skilled electrician, soon got a job, and later Victor did also. Victor did most of the cooking, and all three divided the other household chores.

Throughout these early days in Detroit, Walter, ever the athlete, spent most of his free hours at the YMCA. He soon found that he could play basketball almost as well without his right big toe as he had been able to play with it. For a time, work and the YMCA absorbed all Walter's interest, but Walter, being Walter, always wanted something more.

Valentine Reuther had always impressed upon his sons the value of an education. He was himself largely a self educated man, and it was one of his great regrets that he had not been able to keep his sons in high school and send them on to college. But he had done something that was perhaps more important. He had instilled in them a respect and a desire for learning.

"I decided it was not enough just to keep my body in shape," he says. "It was time I did something about my mind. I decided that the first thing I must do was to finish high school, and so I inquired at the plant whether it would be possible for me to work the afternoon shift steadily. The shifts were usually rotated, but since most men wanted to work days, there wasn't much competition for the shift ending at midnight. They were delighted to oblige me."

Walter then enrolled himself in the Highland Park High School and set up a daily routine that, for years, went like this: he went to work at 3:15 in the afternoon, got off at midnight, hurried home, washed and ate. By 1 A.M. he was ready for study. He usually studied until 4 A.M., got three or four hours sleep, then staggered off groggily to his first class. School took up most of the day, and he got out only barely in time to report for work again.

It was a killing schedule, but Walter handled it with comparative ease. He even had time left over for extracurricular activities. After he had finished high school, he enrolled in Wayne University, where he loaded his schedule with courses in sociology and economics. Already his bent for organizing and leading group action was showing itself.

While he was still in high school, he had formed what he called the 4-C Club. The C's stood for citizenship, comradeship, cooperation, and confidence.

"I had the feeling," Walter explains, "that there were a lot of kids who were having a hard time getting an education, and when they ran into obstacles, they got discouraged and quit. The object of our club was to give them a hand, encourage them, and keep them in school." It was such an obviously worthy cause that the Chamber of Commerce, composed of conservative businessmen, who later would shudder at the mention of Walter Reuther's name, endorsed it and held a big sponsorship rally in a local theater.

When Walter went on to Wayne, his gifts for organization and agitation became even more pronounced. He and his brother, Victor, who enrolled with him, did not have at the time any really clear concept of what they wanted to do in life. They toyed with the idea of becoming lawyers, hung around the courts for a few days, and decided that the justice they saw meted out there was too imperfect a commodity for their tastes.

In this hunt for a more socially useful future, a quest that seems to have been bred in Walter through the ideals inherited from his grandfather and his father, Walter decided to concentrate at Wayne on sociology and economics. These were his two great passions, the two fields of knowledge that, he felt, might lead to that "more socially useful career"; and so he loaded himself up with from 13 to 17 academic credit hours a semester, worked and studied nights, attended school by day, and managed with an average of no more than four hours sleep. And, as if his life wasn't full enough, he pursued his "more socially useful" goal by forming a college Social Service Club.

Walter, naturally, was president of the club, and Victor was one of its officers. Reuther talents dominated the club and quickly made it the gadfly of the college administration. The first battle into which Walter and Victor led their organ- ization was one that would have brought joy to the heart of their grandfather, Jacob Reuther, who had quit Germany in protest against compulsory military training. There was a proposal to make R.O.T.C. at Wayne compulsory for all stu- dents; Walter and Victor and their Social Service Club fought it and eventually defeated it. It was the first victory of many that were to be scored by the combined Reuther talents.

A second and equally notable triumph resulted from a swimming pool controversy. Wayne University, then known as the Detroit City College, was a struggling municipal school holding its classes in what had been the Central High School. Space was strictly limited, and there was of course, much to and distress of its students, no swimming pool and no prospects of getting one. There was great joy among the student body, therefore, when the college administration announced that it had worked out an arrangement with Webster Hall, a large neighboring residential hotel, for the use of its pool by college students during the mornings. Webster Hall, it seemed, had a pool that was much used by its patrons in the afternoons and evenings, but in the mornings it was practically deserted. Putting desertion and need together, the hotel and the college, it seemed, had solved a mutual problem.

"All of the students were excited and delighted," Walter relates. "We all wanted a pool, of course, and now, it seemed, we were going to have one. But then we learned something that chilled our enthusiasm. Under the arrangement the college had concluded with the hotel, the pool was to be segregated—no Negroes were to be allowed. While we all wanted a pool, we didn't want one at that price."

So Walter Reuther, who was later to become expert in such matters, organized his first picket line. Rallying the members of his Social Service Club, he had placards printed denouncing both the hotel and the college, and arming his cohorts with these signs, he threw a picket line of college students about the hotel. The unusual demonstration attracted a lot of attention in the Detroit newspapers and drew down upon the heads of the college administration a volume of unfavorable comment. The swimming pool contract was hastily cancelled, and though the college students lost the chance for a place to swim, Walter Reuther had won his first picket line victory in a battle for a worthwhile principle.

[47]

All during these years, Walter continued to work for Ford. When he was shifted from the Highland Park plant to Ford's huge River Rouge works, he was reputed to be, despite his youth, among the top 25 highest paid mechanics in the entire Ford organization. He was earning $1.45 an hour, and he was sometimes working extra hours on difficult jobs. In those days, with the nation in the pit of the deepest depression it had ever known, with millions of men out of work and the economy collapsing on every side, Walter Reuther was making big money for a working man and had every reason to consider himself extremely fortunate.

He would not have been Walter Reuther, however, had he been satisfied. Beyond Detroit, the whole wide world waited to be explored and investigated, and Walter and Victor talked eagerly about saving their money and setting out on a worker's world tour. Only, of course, Walter, having such a well paying job, could hardly afford to throw it up.

When the Presidential election of 1932 came along, Herbert Hoover, blackened by the worst economic debacle in American history, was the Republican candidate to succeed himself. Franklin D. Roosevelt, who sounded like a conservative Hudson Valley squire and made only vague promises about what he intended to do, was the Democratic candidate. Norman Thomas, who everyone knew didn't have a chance, but who advocated sweeping changes and spoke for a specific program, was the Socialist standard bearer.

Walter Reuther, whose father had run for Congress on the Socialist ticket with Eugene Debs, didn't have to hesitate long in deciding where his allegiance lay. He was for Thomas. This was the kind of heresy for which a man might almost get himself lynched in the ultraconservative Dearborn

[48]

of Henry Ford. Meetings were forbidden; no one was allowed to speak for that Socialist, Norman Thomas. Now, as many men were to discover in later years, to forbid Walter Reuther to do a thing he has set his heart on doing is many times worse than waving a red flag before a bull. Walter becomes only the more determined to accomplish the forbidden feat.

In this case, he quickly evolved a plan. A fellow worker in the Ford plant had persuaded him to make a down payment on a vacant lot a few blocks from the factory, and it occurred to Walter that a man was certainly the lord and master on his own property. Acting on this sound logic, he drove a Ford coupe with a rumble seat into his vacant lot, built a platform across the rumble seat, and clambered up to harangue a gathering crowd on behalf of Norman Thomas.

A lot of jobless men were idle on the streets of Detroit in those days, and they were quickly attracted to any novel spectacle. Soon quite a crowd had gathered. The crowd attracted police. The policemen listened and quickly decided that Walter was a dangerous radical who should be hustled off his impromptu platform. "Listen, bud," one of them told him, "this is private property. You can't speak here."

The grin that lights Walter's face in moments of delicious triumph cast its glow upon his official tormentor. "I know this is private property, officer," he said sweetly. "I own it. Here is the deed." He whipped the document out of his coat pocket and exhibited it triumphantly to the law. There followed several moments of official consternation. After debating how they should act in this unprecedented situation, the gentlemen in blue finally came to a Solomon-like decision. They could not keep Walter from speaking since he was speaking on his own land, but they could limit the size of his audience. This they accomplished by driving four stakes at each corner of the lot. The crowd must stand on the lot.

Walter had won the right to speak for Norman Thomas, but his speaking did neither Thomas nor himself any good. Americans, even in the blackest hours of the Depression, remained an essentially conservative people, and so they swept Roosevelt into office by a landslide. Thomas received little more than a scattered handful of votes.

After the votes were counted came the retribution. Walter, all during the worst days of the Depression, had continued to work steadily at Ford. Now, suddenly, almost overnight, economic conditions became so bad that there was just no job for Walter. Ford was most regretful, but it simply had to lay him off. Typically, Walter Reuther was positively elated. "I came home that night feeling I had been liberated," he says. "I told Vic, 'I've been fired. Now I'm free, and nothing stands in our way. We can go on that trip.'"

The Reuther boys called on their Dean at Wayne University and told him they were leaving school to see the world. "He was so happy he cried," Walter chuckles. "He told us confidentially that he wished he could have been with us in some of our battles, but he had had to carry out the policy of the university. Nevertheless, he was the happiest man in the world to see us go; we were certainly a big load off his mind." All ties to Detroit were now severed except one. Walter went down to the Detroit Bank and drew out $800 he had saved. He got the cash in his hands just in time. Less than a week later, the bank closed. Walter and Victor with two bicycles, and their strong legs, were off to see the world.

Chapter *5*

In the Lands of the Dictators

Germany hit the Reuther brothers like a blow in the face. It was a shock—an incredible, living horror.

They had gone abroad in all innocence, looking upon themselves as students out to learn what they could about labor movements in other countries and to see for themselves how other people lived. They found themselves, almost from the moment they set foot in Europe, caught up in the maelstrom of one of the most brutal and depraved regimes in all human history. Adolf Hitler had just seized power and substituted the rule of his sadistic Nazi Storm Troopers for the laws of the land. Violence and murder reigned.

Before they left for Europe, the Reuthers had equipped themselves with letters of introduction from friends who had relatives and friends abroad. One such letter had been written for them by a professor in Wayne University's German department. It was addressed to a prominent Hamburg businessman. What the professor hadn't known when he wrote the letter was that, since he had last seen his friend, the Hamburg businessman had joined the Nazi Party. Indeed, he had just been given the task of trying to arouse the sympathies and claim the allegiance of Germans and German descendants living in other countries. The arrival of the Reuthers fitted right in with his plans. The Nazi businessman readily envisioned them as two fine lads whom he would convert to Nazism.

No man ever reckoned more incorrectly. To imagine the Reuthers, who had thrown a picket line about a Detroit hotel in protest against swimming pool segregation, embracing a philosophy that contemplated the extermination of the entire Jewish race was sheerest fantasy. Their meeting with the important Nazi was short, hot, and nasty. Inside of ten minutes, the Reuthers had told the wealthy gentleman what they thought of him and were back on the street, still swearing.

Fortunately, they had a second letter of introduction to a Hamburg resident. This was from a Detroit auto mechanic whose uncle lived in the German port city. The uncle, it turned out, was an unemployed dock worker, but he welcomed the Reuthers warmly. They stayed that night at his house, awake most of the time, listening to the gunfire outside. Storm Troopers were riding up and down the streets, shooting at anti-Hitler placards in the windows.

Walter and Victor, after a short stay in Hamburg, boarded a train for Berlin. Sharing their compartment were a worried trade union official—the next day, they learned he had been shot by the Nazis—and two young German workers. The workers were interested in Walter's account of working conditions and trade union activity in America, and one invited them to stay at his house near the railroad station.

When the Reuthers arrived in Berlin, they discovered that the Nazis had just committed the first, monstrous outrage of the Hitler regime. They had burned the Reichstag, home of the German parliament. The ruins were still smoking and smouldering, and the Reuthers took a conducted, Nazi propaganda tour of the site before looking up the address that their friend on the train had given them. It turned out to be a house that served as both shelter and headquarters for a group of anti-Nazi young students and workers.

"We stayed there about ten days," Walter says, "and most of those nights we never took our clothes off. We expected the Storm Troopers to raid the place at any moment, and in fact, just two nights after we left, they did. They wrecked the building and killed all of the students who didn't manage to escape. I'm sure if we had been found there our passports wouldn't have done us much good."

The leader of the young anti-Nazi group, the worker whom the Reuthers had met on the train coming from Hamburg, was Emil Gross. He was one of the fortunate ones who managed to get away, escaping across the Swiss border; but later he slipped back into Germany to work in the anti-Nazi underground. Captured, he was sent to a concentration camp, and the Reuthers supposed he had been murdered until, one day in the winter of 1958, he suddenly turned up in the office of Victor Reuther in Washington. He had survived the Nazi brutality and had become the publisher of one of the leading trade union journals in West Germany.

His reappearance after so long a span, the very fact of his survival, amazed the Reuthers, who had learned themselves at firsthand just how dangerous even the most passive dissent could be in a nation gone wild with race passions and whipped into a constant patriotic frenzy. For even though they were Americans, protected by their passports, they had had rough handling at the hands of Nazi fanatics.

Their first experience occurred in Mannheim, their grandfather's home town. The day before they arrived, a cousin had been arrested and spirited away by the Gestapo, the secret police. The brothers went on to Scharnhausen, their mother's former home. There they saw a worker brutally beaten for protesting the confiscation of his union flag. A few nights later, they took two girl cousins to a movie. The film was a Nazi propaganda picture. After it was over, a swastika flashed on the screen, and the audience rose for the singing of the Nazi anthem, *"Horst Wessel Lied."* Walter, Victor, and the girls, whose father was a typographical worker, remained seated. The audience around them became abusive. Walter waved his passport and protested in English. It cut no ice. He and Victor were cuffed, shoved, and manhandled roughly into the street.

Returning to Berlin, the Reuthers sought visas for Russia. Ford was building a huge factory for the Russians in the city of Gorki; American instructors were needed; and the Reuthers knew that they could get work there. Besides, having seen the Nazi dictatorship first hand, they wanted to get a closeup look at the Russian model. It was not easy, however, to get into Russia; it might take months for their visas to be approved; and so, while they waited for the red tape to be cleared away, the Reuthers set out by bicycle to see what they could of Europe.

They cycled through the Black Forest, toured the old Verdun battlefields where millions of men had been slaughtered in World War I, crossed the border into northern Italy, and visited Austria. They came back, went to England, pedaled through Holland and Belgium, and returned to Germany. All the time, incensed at the Nazi brutalities they had witnessed, they risked their lives carrying messages for the anti-Nazi underground.

"We would leave London, where we had made a contact," Walter recalls, "and we would go to a designated bookstore in a small Ruhr town. We would ask (just as if we were ordinary customers) for a certain very rare, unusual book. The bookseller would tell us, 'I'm sorry, but I don't have the book.' We would pretend surprise. 'But,' we would tell him, 'we were recommended to you. We were told we could buy the book here.' The bookseller would insist he was sorry, there must have been some mistake; he had never carried such a book. 'Well,' we would say then, 'we are very anxious to get this book. Do you know another bookseller who might have it?' Then he would give us a name, and we would go on to the next bookseller and begin all over again. Sometimes, we would make as many as eight contacts in this fashion before finally we reached the person we were supposed to see and delivered our message to.

"When we finally reached the right person, it was a most curious experience. It was amazing the instantaneous bond that seemed to spring up between us, what we felt for him and he for us. They had a feeling toward us, these people, and we for them, as if we had known each other all our lives and been the closest of friends. Yet we had never seen each other before—and probably never would again. It was one of the strangest sensations of my life. It resulted, I suppose, from the fact that we were both engaged in a desperate business, with our lives at stake if we were caught, and this gave both of us a feeling of solidarity—it made you feel in that moment that the man you had made contact with and were talking to was the closest human being in the whole world to you."

In this risky business, the Reuthers never were detected by the totalitarian police, though they had some close calls. On one occasion, when they were in Italy, Victor aroused the ire of the mob and the suspicions of police by taking some pictures of Mussolini during the observance of the Duce's tenth anniversary. And several times, in Germany, the Reuthers' odd conduct piqued official curiosity.

Walter and Victor inevitably drew some attention to themselves because they behaved like no other American tourists the Nazis had ever seen. Tourists always stay in hotels, usually the fancier ones. But the Reuthers never stayed in hotels. They always roomed with the common people, or in youth hostels, or in flophouses that were the last refuge of the unemployed. This was such weird conduct that Storm Troopers sometimes ransacked such quarters just in the hope of discovering what the Reuthers were up to. "Where are those two Americans?" they would demand. Walter and Victor would present themselves, complete with passports. "What are you doing here?" the Storm Troopers would ask suspiciously.

Walter, who was usually the spokesman, would cloak his face in a look of bland surprise. "Why," he would say, "we haven't much money, and we were just looking for a place to sleep for the night. Is there anything wrong with that?" The Storm Troopers would grunt suspiciously, scrutinize the passports, and finally clump away, disgruntled. Fortunately, they never found a clue to indicate to them how valid were their suspicions. The Reuther brothers were very lucky.

Months passed, and still the visas for Russia had not been approved. The Reuthers, short of funds to begin with, were now getting desperate. Walter took a bad spill from his bicycle and cut one arm badly, but they couldn't afford a doctor or a hospital; they bound up the injured arm as best they could and rode on. One night, in France, exhausted and virtually bankrupt, they rode until after nightfall, then dropped their bikes in exhaustion and crawled into what looked like an inviting haystack. When morning came, they found that the stack contained little hay, but much manure.

Finally, the Amtorg Trading Company, the official Russian agency handling tourists' problems in Berlin, notified them that their visas had arrived. It was the dead of winter. In Gorki, the thermometer read 30 degrees below zero. But Walter and Victor had no choice. They needed jobs. Shipping their bicycles ahead, clad only in knickers and jackets and carrying their toolboxes, they set off into the heart of Russia. They were, in Walter's phrase, "completely disorganized." They spoke not a word of Russian. They had only the vaguest idea of how to get where they were going. Fortunately, they met a Red Army officer who put them on the right trolley, and the trolley dropped them in the road a mile-and-a-half from the huge Gorki factory.

As they got off the trolley, one of the other passengers said something and pointed wildly at Walter's jacket. Not understanding a word, Walter looked down. Someone had sliced his jacket open with a knife and deftly lifted his wallet. Luckily, what little cash he had left was in a money belt around his waist, but all the notes he had kept on their

European trip had been stolen. It was a disenchanting initiation to Russia. Worse was to come for the Reuther boys.

After the Reuthers had trudged through the snow and bitter cold to *Amerikanski Pasholik,* the village for American workers, they made a horrifying discovery. The factory in which they would have to labor was unheated. "It was my introduction to the workers' paradise," Walter says dryly. "I still shiver at the memory of that cold," says Victor.

In such surroundings, the Reuthers worked for nearly two years. Walter became a foreman, leading a "brigade" of 16 workers and winning bonuses. But he never became reconciled to the stupidity of the Bolshevik management, which seemed always to be fouling up his production plans, or to the utterly primitive living and working conditions. Safety precautions hardly existed. Meals in the *stalovaya,* the factory lunchroom, usually featured such unappetizing fare as cabbage soup, scooped up with wooden spoons. Equally graphic as an illustration of the almost unbelievable living conditions in Russia was the affair of the metal spoons. Soviet factory bosses had decided to hold a contest. They had come to the conclusion that there wasn't enough culture in the factory, and they decreed that all the workers should think up ways of promoting culture.

The department next to Walter's took an early lead in the contest when it lined its walls with fake palm trees. Walter looked at the palm trees and decided to take a more practical approach. Using fender metal, he machined two barrels of metal spoons. The edges were burred, and if one didn't watch out, he might get a cut lip using them—but they were still metal spoons, to the Russians a positive marvel! The spoons won the contest for Walter's department.

But that was not the end of the story. The spoons were such a novelty, they created such a sensation, that they began to disappear from the dining hall by the barrel full. More spoons were machined from fender metal, but they, too, disappeared almost as fast as they could be made. Finally, in desperation, the factory management passed a stringent rule. Any worker who wanted to eat with one of the Reuther metal spoons would have to surrender his factory pass when the spoon was issued to him. To redeem his pass, he would have to return the spoon.

While such incidents tell their own story about the backwardness and harsh living conditions in Russia, such trials would hardly have prejudiced or discouraged the Reuthers. They were used to hard times, to living on the ragged edge of poverty, and they were not the kind of men to be disenchanted at an encounter with hardships. By the same token, the Reuthers were just the kind of men to be outraged by inhumanity, by brutality; and these were the aspects of the cruel Stalin regime, demonstrated in many tragic episodes during their stay at Gorki, that revolted them and made an indelible impression upon them.

When they first went to Russia, they had open minds about the Communist experiment. Their own and their family's Socialist background predisposed them to believe that probably only exaggerated accounts of Communist brutalities had found their way into the American press and that the reality would prove to be not half so bad as it had been painted. Gorki completely disillusioned them. The principal scene of their disillusionment was the community dining hall; the symbol, the vacant chair whose usual occupant had been spirited away in the night by the Russian secret police. The memory of that vacant chair and what it symbolized has lived in Walter Reuther's mind ever since. Years later, in 1961, he was to describe it in these terms:

"It happened several times while I was there that a family would appear for breakfast without the husband and father.

"When they did so they sat at an isolated table, eyes red from weeping, faces distorted with anxiety and fear. Nobody approached them to ask them what was wrong or where the man of the family was. We all knew. He had been arrested and seized during the middle of the night by the Russian secret police and taken away for imprisonment or to be sent to a work camp in Siberia or even to be executed.

"He was suspected, by the government and the secret police, of political disagreement with the government. Why he was suspected, the family would not know and probably would never learn. They only knew it was highly unlikely they would ever see him again.

"The others in the dining hall knew that any gesture of comfort to the stricken family, even just asking them what had happened, would be interpreted as sympathy, and they might well be the next victims just because of such a gesture."

Walter Reuther never forgot such heartrending spectacles. They were a major reason that, after he returned to America, he became one of the bitterest foes of the Communists in the American labor movement.

Nearly two years of labor in the primitive surroundings of Gorki replenished the Reuthers' finances enough for them to be able to move on and see more of the world. Setting out on their bicycles, they pedaled 22,000 miles through central

Asia and Siberia, living on less than 50 cents a day. "We lived out in the desert with nomadic tribesmen north of Persia and slept in their goatskin tents," Walter recalls. "We lived with peasants, coal miners, steelworkers. Basically, we were learning about people, and the thing we learned is that the outer shell of man is quite different, but inside they are all exactly alike. They all want the same things—sufficient food and shelter and security for their families; peace in the world and a better life, better opportunities, for their children than they have had. These are the things that all men want, and what we found out by living with all kinds of people, sharing their tents on the desert, going down into the coal mines with them, is that the good in man is so much more overwhelming than the bad.

"That is why I don't buy war. I don't believe the negative reflexes of fear and hatred represent man's greatest aspirations. But we have never given man a chance. We have never worked out a rule, a system, that would give a whole generation of the world's youth the chance to live and work together in peace with the kind of dedication we give to war. When that day comes, there is no limit to what man can achieve."

It was a philosophy whose seeds doubtless were planted in those Sunday family debates in Valentine Reuther's home in Wheeling, but a philosophy for which Walter Reuther found confirmation by living with tribesmen and peasants on the plains of Asia.

He and Victor were in Tashkent when they decided that the time had come for them to conclude their world tour by pressing on to China, the Pacific, and home. To get out of Russia, however, they had to return to Moscow so that their passports could be processed, and they had to obtain passage on the Trans-Siberian Railroad that would take them across the whole vast continent of Asia on their way to the East. They traveled, of course, the cheapest way, third class. They were on the train 13 days and 13 nights. Their only beds were hard oaken boards. Their companions, except for one engaging and highly articulate Englishman who was traveling first class, were Russian peasants, and their principal refreshment was the tea that they and the peasants brewed and shared together. As they went farther East, Mongolian faces began to mix with the white Russian faces at the stations through which they passed.

"It is the oddest sensation," Reuther remembers. "There seems to be no line where the Caucasian race ends and the Mongolian begins. As you go farther East, you see more and more Mongolian faces sprinkled in the crowds—it's a sort of slow, even blend—and then, the next morning, the train stops at a small city, and you look out, and you see nothing but this sea of Mongolian faces. They're all over the place, as if they had sprung up out of the ground during the night, and you know that you're in the Far East at last."

At the stops along the way, the Reuthers had become quite friendly with the pleasant Englishman. He was, he said, Haley Bell, a retired English officer who had gone into the manufacture of aluminum in Japan. Victor Reuther describes him as "the spitting image of C. Aubrey Smith," and neither he nor Walter had any idea that kindly, courteous Haley Bell had any special reason for being interested in them. When they stopped and stretched their legs on station platforms, he chatted to them about their experiences in Gorki and chuckled at their youthful idealism and their faith in

[62]

the brotherhood of man. It did seem perhaps a bit peculiar that Haley Bell kept bringing the conversation back to the topic of Gorki, pumping them for the last item of their knowledge about the great Volga factory, but this they put down at the time to idle curiosity. It was not until after World War II that British Prime Minister Winston Churchill disclosed to the House of Commons—and to the astonished Reuthers—that Britain's top secret service agent in the Far East throughout the prewar years had been Lieut. Col. Haley Bell.

The disclosure solved a mystery for the Reuthers. They had never been able to understand why, the moment they reached Manchuria, the Japanese secret police had been so suspicious of them. On one occasion, they had been held two days for questioning, and they hadn't had the faintest idea what it had been all about. Now, long years later, all became clear. Obviously, Japanese intelligence had had its own suspicions about Lieut. Col. Haley Bell and anyone who associated with the courtly Englishman instantly became suspect. Having no suspicion of this at the time, the Reuthers had been far more concerned at Haley Bell's callous attitude toward poor coolie labor. There was a long stopover in Mukden, and Haley Bell proposed that they hire rickshas. "Come on," he said, "I'll show you the city."

"What?" Walter cried. "Be carried around by another human being? Not on your life!"

"Silly ass," Haley Bell muttered, leaving the Reuthers to their own devices.

True to their principles, the Reuthers shook off the eager ricksha boys and set out to see what they could see on foot. Late in the day, tired and hot, Walter heard someone calling his name. He whirled around and was startled to see Haley Bell coming along the street, sitting erect in a ricksha, immaculately dressed in a white linen suit and pith helmet. As his bearer sped him past the astonished Reuthers, he doffed his pith helmet and intoned, "Behold the British imperialist!"

It was the last they saw of Haley Bell, for his route and theirs now diverged. He was going to Shanghai; they, to Peiping, and so he passed out of their lives. But he left behind him the disturbing residue of an ethical problem. Should anyone who believed in the equality and brotherhood of man ever consent to being hauled around by another human being?

The question haunted the Reuthers when they arrived in Peiping. There they found some 20 ricksha boys lined up, eagerly soliciting their patronage. True to their convictions, the Reuthers refused to be hauled in rickshas, but everywhere they went, ricksha boys followed them, waited for them, vied for their trade. Times were hard in China, and ricksha-pullers needed every fare they could get. They had a saying: "White man, he got money, no patience. We got no money, lots of patience." The patience finally wore down the Reuthers' principles. One letter of introduction was to the president of a university about 13 miles outside Peiping. The only really practical way to make the trip was to travel by ricksha, and so Walter and Victor, reluctantly surrendering, hired two rickshas to carry them.

Even though practicality had dictated their action, they were still greatly disturbed about it. They felt it just wasn't right to be transported in such fashion, and so, after a few miles, they hit upon a device to salve their consciences.

[64]

Ordering a halt, they got out, ordered the ricksha boys into their comfortable seats, put themselves between the shafts, and started out along the road. "They thought we were nuts," Walter confesses, "but we persuaded them, got them in, and pulled them down the road at a smart pace for awhile." But only for awhile. The Reuthers soon discovered that the ricksha boys were more adept at hauling rickshas than they were, and so it wasn't long before they were persuaded to resume their seats and finish their journey in style.

This amusing interlude was followed by one of the most harrowing and horrifying experiences of their trip. To get to the Chinese coast, they engaged passage on a Yangtze River steamer. The Yangtze at the time was in full flood, rice crops had been destroyed, and the Chinese in the countryside through which they passed were starving. In the streets of the river towns, parades of children, beating tin cans and begging food, followed all foreigners. Everyone knew there would be food, there would be rice, on the river steamer; and when it left Hankow, starving men, trying to leap aboard, were clubbed to death by burly Sikh deck hands and tossed into the swirling river waters. Farther down the stream, the vessel rammed and sank a Chinese junk. Some 40 persons aboard the junk drowned before the Reuthers' eyes as the captain of the steamer watched indifferently. When Walter angrily protested and demanded that an effort be made to rescue the victims, the captain simply shrugged his shoulders and turned away, muttering that these crazy Americans didn't understand China. In China, human life was one of the cheapest commodities.

With this nightmarish experience behind them, the Reuthers finally reached Japan. In Yokohama they took stock of their resources. They had only $7 between them, and they were 7,000 miles from home. Seeking help, they reported to the American consulate, and the consul found them berths in the crew of the cruise liner *President Harding*. So they worked their way back home across the vast Pacific, Victor spending his days pleasantly enough polishing brass and chatting with the first-class passengers, Walter toiling and sweating in the engine room.

In California, they got their sea pay and spent it to buy bus tickets back to Wheeling, West Virginia. They had been gone nearly three years—gone so long that, when they telephoned ahead to let their family know they were coming, their father at first did not recognize their voices.

Chapter **6**

Union Beginnings

Walter and Victor Reuther got back home just in time. The domestic scene in America was changing, and for the first time in the history of the automobile industry, an effective labor organization was about to be born.

The changes stemmed from the New Deal administration of President Roosevelt and its encouragement of effective union organization. Unions, which had been hampered by restrictive laws that rendered them virtually powerless, were to grow within a few short years into a mighty force in American life, and nowhere was the impact of this startling turn about to be felt more strongly than in Detroit. There the automobile industry had always gone to extreme lengths to maintain the open shop and to keep the workers on its assembly lines in complete subjection.

To understand the Detroit that was about to be torn by labor warfare unprecedented in its history, one has to understand the Detroit that Walter Reuther had left for his trip abroad and the Detroit to which he returned. It was a Detroit whose brutality toward the men who labored in its auto factories can hardly be overestimated. The inhuman speedup on its assembly lines drove men to the utter limits of physical endurance and at times almost to the borders of insanity. Louis-Ferdinand Céline, the French novelist who labored in Detroit for a time, later wrote this unforgettable description of life in the auto factories:

"One was turned by force into a machine oneself, the whole of one's carcass quivering in this vast frenzy of noise, which filled you within and all around the inside of your skull and lower down rattled your bowels, and climbed to your eyes in infinite, little, quick unending strokes . . . you long to stop and hear your heart beating clearly within you; but now it's impossible. I can't stop . . . The workmen bending solicitously over the machines eager to keep them happy, are a depressing sight; one hands them the right-sized screws and still more screws, instead of putting a stop once and for all to all this smell of oil, and this vapor which burns your throat and your eardrums from inside . . . When at six o'clock everything stops, you carry the noise away in your head. I had a whole night's noise and smell of oil in mine, as if I'd been fitted with a new nose . . . my mates were mere echoes and whiffs of machinery like myself, flesh shaken up for good."

Men who endured these conditions lived for the most part on the ragged edge of poverty and with the swords of dictatorial and ruthless managements dangling precariously above their heads. For years, caught in a trap from which there seemed no escape, men dared not open their mouths or take one step in their own defense, afraid that their sim-

[68]

plest gesture might deprive them of the miserable livelihood that they had.

The psychological scars grew deep on the souls of men on the assembly lines. The first scar tissue had formed in that horrible winter of 1927 when Walter Reuther first came to Detroit. Ford, in the shift-over from Model T to Model A, had layed off 100,000 men. Many of them were unemployed from six months to more than a year. In that time, they and their families almost starved to death, and none of them ever forgot it. Not only the Ford workers themselves, but workers on every assembly line in the city paid the penalty. With this many men roaming the streets looking for jobs, with others constantly flocking in from the countrysides of several surrounding states, factory bosses were in the driver's seat and became completely ruthless. They speeded up the assembly lines to tempos never previously achieved; they drove the helpless human cattle who tended them to maintain the stepped-up pace; and if a man protested, he was speedily reminded that, if he didn't want his job, there were a thousand others outside who did.

The process of speedup and virtual enslavement on the assembly line that began with the Ford changeover was intensified by the cruel, unremitting pressures of the Depression. Not only was business bad, impelling auto magnates to further speedups and further cutting of costs, but a permanent excess labor force gathered and waited at the employment gate of every plant, eager for even a single day's work. The waiting throngs of the unemployed would assemble by 6 A.M., trying to warm themselves in the cold by small bonfires, and they would wait and wait until plant foremen came out and picked whomever they wanted. Seniority, experience, didn't mean a thing. All that counted was whether a man was a young and willing beast who could be driven fast.

The hopelessness underlying such experiences was expressed in cold statistics. In 1929 slightly more than 470,000 men were employed in Detroit's auto factories. By 1933 less than half this number were employed, and they were working for far less, earning only one-third of the wages paid in 1929. These were the fortunate ones, the lucky ones who were actually making, on an average, $17.57 a week. The unlucky accumulated on Detroit's relief rolls and eked out a pitiful existence. Their erstwhile employers made no move to help them and expressed, indeed, complete indifference to their fate. In March 1932, when a number of unemployed Ford workers gathered at the River Rouge plant to dramatize their plight, Ford guards and Dearborn police, who could always be counted upon to back up Ford, dispersed them with gunfire. Four demonstrators were shot dead; many more were wounded.

In 1935, just at the time Walter Reuther returned to Detroit, one of the most intensive studies ever made of the automobile industry was released. It was the work of Leon Henderson, a government economist, who had made the detailed report for NRA, the National Recovery Administration. Henderson described the workers' attitude:

"The fear of layoff is always in their minds, even if not definitely brought there by the foremen. The speedup is thus inherent in the present situation of lack of steady work and an army of unemployed waiting outside . . .

"The automobile industry has set a new low age for displacement of workers. Men near forty find great difficulty in securing jobs with the industry or being rehired after layoffs.

"There was bitter opposition to the group piecework and the group bonus plans which were devised to drive them to excessive speed. . . .

"Labor unrest exists to a degree higher than warranted by the depression. The unrest follows from insecurity, low annual earnings, inequitable hiring and rehiring methods, espionage, speed-up and displacement of workers at an extremely early age . . . Unless something is done soon, they [the workers] intend to take things into their own hands to get results."

The great automobile firms met this threat, which Henderson so accurately and perceptively described, not by trying to correct wrongs and better conditions, but by hiring private armies and instituting campaigns of espionage, terror, and suppression. The Henderson report noted that, in one two-and-a-half year period, General Motors had paid the Pinkerton Detective Agency $419,000 and Chrysler had paid another private detective firm $211,000. These sums, huge as they were, were soon to be dwarfed. Soon, in a comparable period, General Motors was to be spending nearly $1,000,000 for plant espionage, and Henry Ford was to raise a private army of 3,000 gangsters and plug-uglies whom he was to arm with machine guns.

Such were the unequal forces that were virtually in the trenches, lined up for combat, when Walter Reuther returned to Detroit. The forces, by any expression of power, were most unevenly matched. On the one side, there was the helpless mass of fearful but increasingly desperate men, lacking organization, lacking leadership and resources; on the

[71]

other, the arrayed might of the motor magnates with their hired armies, their private detectives, their omnipresent spies—and, above all, their iron determination to keep Detroit an open shop city, one in which no labor union should ever be permitted to gain a foothold. It looked like a most uneven contest, but there could be no question where Walter Reuther's sympathies lay. He had been born on labor's side of the tracks, and he was almost fanatically proud of the fact.

Even before he had been fired by Ford in 1932, he had been agitating for the formation of a union, but he had made little headway. The men had been too fearful; the time had not been right. Reuther tells about these early unionizing efforts with a wry humor. Ford, he explains, had not cut wages as early in the Depression as the other companies. For several years, Ford kept its original pay scale, but finally, shortly before Reuther was fired for his Socialist and union activities, the fateful day arrived.

"Our superintendent lined us up and told us: 'Beginning today, we're cutting your rates five cents an hour,'" Reuther relates. "I don't know, but I expect that they were anticipating trouble, they were testing us to see how we would take it. But there was no revolution. The men took it quietly.

"So after the lunch hour, when we came back to work, the superintendent lined us all up again and told us we were being cut another five cents an hour. That's what really made the men sore. If they'd cut us ten cents an hour to begin with, it wouldn't have made half the impression, but cutting us five cents before lunch and five cents afterwards, after it had become obvious we were too helpless to do anything about it, was an outright insult. It made the men furious.

"I remember there were three deaf mute brothers who worked in my department. I had learned enough of their sign language to communicate with them a bit, and I had been talking up the need for us to form a union. But I hadn't been getting anywhere. Well, after the first pay cut was announced, I remember the youngest of them slipped me a note. It read: 'At the lunch hour, let's start the revolution.' "

Not many men at Ford were yet ready for the revolution, however, and so, after lunch, they had to swallow the second pay cut. And shortly afterwards, of course, Reuther himself drew a pink dismissal slip and, with his brother Victor, was off to Europe and a trip around the world to see what the world of labor was doing.

While he was gone, several futile efforts had been made at unionization. All had foundered more or less disastrously. One of the major causes for the repeated failures was the ineptness of the American Federation of Labor, the only large labor organization in America at the time, and the lethargy and timidity of its president, William Green, whom the auto workers came to dub with contempt, "Sitting Bill." Despite the failures, despite the inadequacy of A. F. of L. leadership, the men on the assembly lines were growing desperate. Walter Reuther, coming up to Detroit from Wheeling in the winter of 1935, quickly sensed the change in attitude, quickly felt what he calls "a sense of little people marching."

The indifference that had frustrated him at Ford in 1932 was gone. There was now passion and faith. The workers even had a hymn that they sang with fervor. It was one they had resurrected from the days when Valentine Reuther's hero, "Big Bill" Haywood, had led his International Work-

ers of the World into labor battles. It was called, "Solidarity
Forever"; and it went, in part, like this:

"When the union's inspiration through the worker's blood
  shall run
"There can be no greater power anywhere beneath the
  sun . . ."

To find workers singing this militant air was, for Walter
Reuther, to breathe air like wine. Very much his father's
son, he could hardly wait to get into the battle, and he
promptly set about organizing a small union local. Today,
looking back, he remembers those strife-torn years of the
late 1930's with the nostalgia of a man of advancing age for
his fighting youth; they remain to him a time when he was
young "and the world was simple, and there was a frontier
ahead."

Walter Reuther was determined to cross that frontier
as one of the leaders of the newborn labor movement. As a
union organizer, he was not exactly welcome in the automobile plants of Detroit, but he made a living by doing
occasional tool and die work in small factories and by serving
as a recreation director for the Works Progress Administration. Walter at the moment didn't mind. Life was all in the
future, and it was a future that was being brightened by the
presence of a girl whom he began to meet regularly on a
Detroit streetcar. She was May Wolf, a young school teacher,
and she confided to Walter that she was trying to get her
fellow teachers to organize. It was a beautiful meshing of
mutual interests. Almost every night May and Walter met on
the streetcar and discussed unions and the news of develop-

ments in the labor movement until she had to get off the streetcar.

After three months of this kind of shop talk, May and Walter decided that there were, after all, other things in life than unions. On March 13, 1936, they were married. Right after the ceremony, they left Detroit, but not on the kind of honeymoon most brides and grooms envision. Walter had to address a labor rally in Mount Clemens that night.

Back in Detroit in the spring of 1936, Walter was determined to attend the first convention of the newly formed United Automobile Workers at South Bend, Indiana. The union had been organized the year before under A. F. of L. jurisdiction, and "Sitting Bill" Green hadn't even asked its members whom they wanted for a leader. He had simply picked and installed one of his own palace-guard stooges. The chieftain Green had given the UAW had quickly proved himself a bumbler, and now the auto workers, completely fed up, were determined to shed the A. F. of L. yoke for good. Walter wanted to have a hand in the shedding.

He had, however, a major problem. His union local was almost nonexistent. Workers were still so fearful of reprisals in the auto plants that many of them did not dare to come to meetings; and when Walter called a session to pick a delegate to the UAW convention, only seven members showed up. Not surprisingly, the seven picked Walter to represent them. Officially named a delegate, Walter promptly faced other, practical problems. He had no money; neither did his union. The treasurer of the local gave Walter $5—all the money the treasury contained—and Walter set out to hitch-hike the 175 miles to South Bend. Arriving there, he shared a room with five other delegates and lived on hamburgers.

The South Bend convention, held on April 27, 1936, severed all UAW ties with the A. F. of L. and named its own president. He was Homer L. Martin, then 34, a former Baptist preacher who had worked briefly in the auto plants, had become overnight an ardent unionist, and had become noted for a revivalist flow of oratory that could work men up to a steaming, fighting pitch. The other officers were Wyndham Mortimer, a cagey and veteran unionist, vice-president; and George Addes, already known for his toughness and shrewdness as the result of his leadership role in an Autolite strike in Toledo, secretary-treasurer. Among the delegates chosen to sit on the executive board was a chunky, compactly build redhead who was already becoming the favorite of Detroit's West Side locals—Walter Reuther. For a young man who had come to South Bend representing a barely breathing local, it was a great personal triumph.

The new UAW leadership promptly decided to affiliate with John L. Lewis' Committee for Industrial Organization, later the Congress of Industrial Organizations. The beetle-browed Lewis, originally head of the United Mine Workers, had set up the CIO to organize all workers in given industries, the skilled and the unskilled, instead of following the A. F. of L. pattern of organizing individual crafts. Though the CIO was still a part of the A. F. of L., Lewis ran his own show and was already on his way out of the parent organization. He agreed to finance the UAW in its organizing drive in Detroit to the extent of $100,000.

Considering the size of the job to be done, this money represented little more than peanuts. It certainly didn't help Walter Reuther. He had in his pockets only what was left of the $5 with which he had started out, and he had to hitchhike his way back home from South Bend. Once more in Detroit, he decided to borrow $300 to get his local moving. With the money, he hired a sound truck, rented an office, and moved in a secondhand desk, a mimeograph machine, a typewriter—and Mrs. Walter Reuther. May had been making $60 a week as a teacher; her husband now paid her $15 as a secretary—and saw that she endorsed even this pittance right back to the union. She was, Walter acknowledges wryly, "the lowest-paid secretary in the city."

Since Walter himself was drawing no salary from the union, the finances of the young couple were almost non-existent. To make ends meet, they moved into the small La Salle Boulevard apartment of May's parents. But they were rarely at home. Almost every night Walter was speaking at a union meeting, and May was with him. Usually, it was 10:30 before they stopped off at some cheap restaurant for a skimpy supper. "I never knew people to eat less," May said years afterwards. "I was so thin the mattress hurt my hips."

Those were hard times for the Reuthers, but they were challenging times, too. The redhead had a flair for speaking, and, undeniably, he was beginning to make his way. It was not perhaps so much what he said as the dynamic quality, the conviction in the way he said it. He had an almost missionary zeal when he spoke about people and their problems. His mind was lightning fast; he always seemed to have the latest facts and figures at his fingertips; ability seemed stamped all over him. The auto workers, cheered by the split with the A. F. of L., feeling that under the new CIO regime they might get somewhere, were looking for just such a leader, and they became increasingly enamored with Walter Reuther. More men constantly joined his local, and

[77]

soon several other West Side locals merged with it, forming powerful Local 174, with Walter as its president.

Prospects were improving but almost as soon as they started to improve, they dimmed again. Walter had been working as a tool and die maker in a small factory. One afternoon, his foreman inspected the die he was making and congratulated him on a fine job. Walter, never the bashful type, promptly asked for a raise—and got it. At 7 o'clock the next morning, when he reported for work, he was told that his salary was being raised a dime an hour; at 9 o'clock the same morning, he was notified that he was being fired for incompetence. Nobody troubled to explain how he could have been so good he was worth ten cents more an hour at 7 o'clock and so bad two hours later that it was necessary to fire him. But, obviously, somebody had heard that sound truck, and, obviously, the firm wanted no such union agitator in its midst. Neither did other firms in Detroit. Walter, leaving the plant and looking for other work, found that this time he had been most thoroughly and efficiently blacklisted. There was, for him, no job in all Detroit. The blacklisting came at a most inopportune time, for Walter Reuther had plans—plans for his first big strike—and he needed a job inside the target plant to make sure the plans worked.

Nearly half of the members of Walter's Local 174 worked at the Kelsey-Hayes Wheel Corporation, makers of brakes for Ford. These workers had been complaining about speedups that drove them to the limit of endurance, and Walter had tried to discuss their complaints with management. But management had given him the rough back of its hand. It said Walter didn't represent the workers, and it wasn't going to talk with him. And so Walter had been planning a demonstration to convince management that he did represent the men and that it was going to have to talk.

The technique he had in mind was not new, though it was comparatively novel in America. It was the sit-down strike. Sit-downs had been tried first in Europe. Two years before, Welsh and Hungarian miners had refused to come out of the mines until their wages were raised. In the United States in November 1935, workers at the Goodyear plant in Akron had sat-down on the job until a grievance was settled. A few weeks later, the same thing happened at a Firestone plant. Walter was convinced that the technique that had worked in rubber would work equally well in autos. All that was needed was for enough men to sit-down at the same time; once the workers stopped tending those fast moving assembly lines, chaos would be almost instantaneous.

But to organize such a demonstration right, to make sure it didn't misfire, Walter himself needed to be on the scene, working at a job inside the embattled plant. And with the blacklisting against him, he knew he didn't have a chance. In this crisis, he turned to his brother, Victor. After their return from Europe, Victor had become a lecturer for the Quaker Emergency Peace Program and had given several talks at Brookwood Labor College. Among his students was a bright-eyed scholarship winner named Sophie. They had only recently been married, and Victor, accompanied by his bride, was still on the road talking for the Quakers when he received a summons from Walter. Victor listened to him explain the situation by long-distance phone, then told Sophie they would have to pack and travel. The following afternoon saw him back in Detroit, and a few hours later he was working at a punch press in Kelsey-Hayes for $36\frac{1}{2}$ cents an hour.

With Victor on the scene, Walter called a strategy meeting at the La Salle Boulevard apartment. He had expected most of the 78 unionists he had registered in Kelsey-Hayes to attend, but so fearful were the men of reprisals for union activity that only 15 showed up. Almost all of these, however, worked on the critical brake-assembly line, the part of the plant most affected by the speedup.

Walter realized that what he could not accomplish by strength he would have to achieve by clever stratagem. "We had a big Polish gal at the meeting who had fainted on the assembly line once before," he explains. "We assigned her to 'faint' again, and showed her how to do it. That was to be the signal. When she 'fainted,' someone else was to shut down the assembly line. We trained a couple of men in pulling the right switches."

Victor Reuther was at work at a punch press on the floor below the brake-assembly line when Walter's plans were carried into action. Everything worked like well oiled machinery. One instant Victor was stamping out a new piece every ten seconds; the next, he heard an uproar on the floor above. The Polish girl had "fainted," the selected workmen had pulled the key switches on the brake-assembly line, and collaborators were shouting, "Strike! Strike" at the top of their lungs.

Victor abandoned his punch press, raced upstairs, found a packing case and climbed up on it. When the first uproar had died down, he was haranguing the fainthearts among the factory's 5,000 workers and urging them to join the union. A bewildered personnel man, plucking at his cuff, suggested that he ought to devote his talents instead to getting the men back to work.

"Only Walter Reuther can do that," said Victor.

"Who's Walter Reuther?" asked the personnel man. He was quickly enlightened.

During these minutes of fast paced action inside Kelsey-Hayes, Walter sat impatiently at the desk in his cubbyhole office, watching the ticking hands of his watch and waiting for the telephone call that would tell him whether he had succeeded or failed. Finally, it came. It was from the Kelsey-Hayes' front office; they wanted him to come over to their factory and restore peace.

"What makes you think I can help you?" Walter inquired blandly. "You told me I don't represent the workers."

"If anybody can do it, you can," the management voice assured him. The voice added that a company car was being sent to speed him to the plant.

Walter rode to Kelsey-Hayes in style, was escorted by management through the gates that had been barred to him, and mounted Victor's packing case. Then he took up right where Victor had left off, urging the workers who didn't belong to join the union. This wasn't at all what management had bargained for. The horrified personnel man twiched Walter's pant leg. "You're supposed to get them back to work, not organize them," he said.

Walter, eyes dancing, a grin on his face, looked down and inquired innocently: "But how can I get them back to work if they're not organized?"

Management was nonplussed, but stubborn. The sitdowners, led by the Reuthers, were stubborn, too. They sat and occupied the plant for five days and five nights, sustained by a food supply system that Walter climbed out a window to organize. Then management caved in. It signed a contract recognizing the union and granting a pay hike to a minimum of 75 cents an hour. It was one of the most dramatic triumphs the auto workers had scored, one of the first times in America that sit-downers had actually taken over and occupied a plant for an extended period until their battle was won. Membership application cards flooded Walter's office, and in less than six months membership zoomed to 2,400. It was merely a taste of the tests and triumphs to come.

Chapter 7

Cracking General Motors and Ford

W alter Reuther's triumph at Kelsey-Hayes was like the sudden release of a compressed spring. It twanged and vibrated, and almost instantly labor broke out in a sit-down rash. Reuther had shown the way, and workers in a spontaneous chain reaction that speaks loudly of the long suppressed, underlying pressures, rushed to copy his successful method. Union leaders no longer had to work to sell the idea of union membership to labor; labor, in a great many instances, called its own strikes and then rushed to join the union.

"A guy we never heard of would call up and say, 'We shut down such-and-such a plant. Send us over some coffee and doughnuts,'" Reuther says. "So we'd send over the stuff. Later on, we'd organize central kitchens and mobile feeding units. Our organizing committee was in session continuously. We slept hardly at all. That's how we grew. It was a real industrial revolution."

Revolution was, indeed, the proper word for it, and as is the case with revolutions, it could hardly be peaceful. With workers calling their own spontaneous strikes and then begging to be taken into the UAW, orderly and responsible planning became almost impossible. Reuther and the other leaders in the forefront of the movement had caught a tiger by the tail, and even if they had wished, which they didn't, they probably could not have stopped the angry beast from lashing out with his claws. The explosive eruption in the auto plants that Leon Henderson had predicted was now living reality.

The first tremendous upheaval from the seething pit of labor rocked the titan of the industry and, by its violence, shocked the nation. It was the spontaneously called, runaway strike against General Motors. The UAW had been trying throughout 1936 to organize GM. In its campaign to persuade workers to join the union, it had hammered away at a few basic arguments. "The year in which GM's profits were $228,000,000, the worker's average wage was slightly over $1,100," it proclaimed. "Between January, 1934, and July, 1936, the corporation spent close to $1,000,000 for plant espionage. Speedups again and again. . . ."

Using such arguments, Wyndham Mortimer, the UAW vice-president, headed an organizing team that tried to lure workers in General Motors plants in Flint into the union. Mortimer first tried to clean out company spies who had worked their way into key spots in the locals, but General Motors had not spent $1,000,000 for plant espionage in vain. Its hired agents within the locals, by raising false issues and making false charges, kept the membership in such a state of discord that nothing could be accomplished. Spies

[84]

posing as ardent unionists even turned some of the locals against the organizers by labeling the organizers Communist agitators. Mortimer, who appears to have been vulnerable on the issue, was so discredited that by this attack he was driven out of Flint.

Robert Travis and Roy Reuther, the first of the Reuther brothers to become a fully paid union official, succeeded him and carried on the organizing campaign. Travis managed to expose some of the informers, and he and Roy Reuther won the allegiance of rank-and-file union men. Steadily, they built up the strength of the Flint locals, preparing for the day when they would be strong enough for an effective contract showdown with the giant General Motors.

The coming of this day was constantly being speeded by the conduct of the men themselves. They were in no mood to wait. The speedup had become so fatiguing that, at the end of a shift, many men were too exhausted to participate in home activities; they could only collapse. Resentful, the men began to call wildcat strikes on their own. The last half of 1936 was marked by a number of sporadic work stoppages in the Chevrolet and Fisher Body plants in Flint. Each was quickly settled, and the workers, feasting on such minor victories, become encouraged, emboldened, and impatient.

Barely contained, the unrest built swiftly until it finally exploded in a violent crisis at the end of December 1936. On December 18, William Knudsen, General Motors president, in rejecting a union demand, seemed to leave the door just a bit ajar. He protested that GM had no intention of "discouraging" union organization, agreed that he felt "collective bargaining is here to stay," but insisted it "ought to take place before a shutdown rather than after."

Homer Martin, UAW's preacher-president, rushed into the breach and asked for a conference on such matters as speedup, discrimination, job security, and the abuse of piece-work rates. General Motors agreed to see union representatives, but only on a plant-by-plant basis. Since general policy for the entire organization was set at the top and individual plant bosses had no choice but to carry it out, the UAW felt such piecemeal negotiations would be prolonged and useless, and refused to participate in them. There now occurred the briefest of pauses. Union leaders were not certain of their strength in the auto plants. In addition, CIO chieftain John L. Lewis did not want to become embroiled at this time in a major showdown in the auto industry; his strategy called instead for a drive to organize steel first. But the men in the plants were in no mood to wait longer. Feeling their strength, aroused and wrathful, they acted without consulting the leadership.

On December 28, provoked by a long string of unsettled grievances, the workers of the Cleveland Fisher Body plant halted production by sitting down at their jobs. The next day, the men in Flint's Fisher Body Plant No. 2 joined the movement after the manager fired five union spokesmen for requesting collective bargaining. The next night, workers in the more important Fisher Body Plant No. 1 noticed that vital dies were being placed on freight cars for shipment. Recognizing that if the dies were shipped GM might be able to set up production elsewhere, Travis consulted with the unionized workers and pointed out to them that they would have to halt the shipment if they wanted to save their jobs.

The men at once voted to sit-down and not to leave the plant until the dispute was settled. By New Year's Eve, both Flint plants were occupied by the sit-downers, and the crucial battle of the sit-downs was joined.

Lewis, his primary objective still the organization of steel, had tried at first to prevent the sit-downs from spreading, but he quickly saw that this was impossible. Lewis recognized that the strike now would have either to be completely won or completely lost, and so he threw all the resources of the CIO behind it.

The battle lines, bitterly drawn at the start, quickly stiffened until the strike assumed the aspect of a civil war. The major battleground was the city of Flint. The birthplace of the Buick Company, Flint had some 165,000 residents, of whom approximately 50,000 worked in the auto plants. The central Fisher Body plants and the major Chevrolet factories were located there. If these key Flint plants could be closed down, all GM would be slowed almost to a standstill.

All Flint, labor charged—its city officials, its police, its newspapers, and its radio station—belonged body and soul to GM. Soon events seemed to indicate that there was more than a little truth to the charge. On January 4, 1937, General Motors rejected every union demand, began a back-to-work campaign, and asked federal action to clear the plants of the strikers. It rushed into a state court, and from Circuit Judge Edward D. Black, of Flint, obtained an injunction ordering the strikers to leave the plants and refrain from picketing. This was a strikebreaking judicial decree if it was allowed to stand, but union lawyers didn't let it stand. They looked into Judge Black's background and found he owned $219,000 worth of GM stock. Since Michigan law prohibits a jurist from sitting in a case in which he has a personal interest, the strikebreaking injunction was voided, and unfavorable publicity boomeranged on GM.

Neither this black eye nor the collapse of its first legal offensive deterred General Motors. It backed the formation of the "Flint Alliance," headed by George Boysen, a former Buick paymaster who had become the owner of a small spark-plug factory. A highly paid New York public relations man was imported, and a high-pressure campaign was started to blacken the reputation of the union and whip up local support for GM. Boysen got the cooperation of the city manager, police officials, and anti-union citizens; and he was joined by a large number of workers who had not belonged to the UAW when the strike started and wanted to return to their jobs at any price. Uniting these forces, Boysen and his New York public relations man accused UAW officials of Communism and racketeering, blasted the "invasion" of Flint by outside agitators, and called upon public-spirited citizens to rise and drive these interlopers—except for the New York public relations man, of course—right out of the city. This militant plan, if followed, could lead only to a frightful and bloody clash.

The UAW, recognizing that its very life was at stake, rallied its legions from all over the Midwest area. From Detroit, Cleveland, Toledo, and Akron, thousands of union activists poured into the strike-beleaguered city of Flint. One of the most powerful delegations came from Detroit's West Side locals, headed by Walter and Victor Reuther, with their sound truck in the van.

With opposing armies marshalled in such strength, the inevitable happened. On the afternoon of January 11, 1937, management shut off the heat in Fisher 1. A few hours later, in what had every appearance of a concerted action, Flint police surrounded the entrance of the plant and announced no further shipments of food would be permitted. A ladder placed against a window by strikers in an attempt to smuggle food into the sit-downers was instantly torn down. Dinner time came on this bitterly cold day, and the police still maintained their positions, while inside the plant the sit-downers shivered and went hungry.

In the early evening, Victor Reuther charged upon the scene with a sound truck. Scores of unionists soon surrounded it. Victor, taking the microphone, pleaded with police to let the food shipments through. The police didn't give any sign they had heard him. His appeal failing, Victor then began to broadcast a fighting exhortation to the workers inside the plant and out. Soon he had the men whipped up into a fighting temper, and at 7 P.M., in a concerted rush, unionists charged the plant gates from both sides, swept the police aside, and carried coffee, bread, and other food into the plant.

The police, temporarily vanquished, soon returned to the fray. At 9 o'clock, 50 of them, more than half of Flint's entire police force, charged the pickets guarding the plant entrance. They clubbed some, scattered others. A policeman shattered the glass pane of a door, poked a tear-gas gun through the opening and fired it. The gassed strikers inside fell back, and police, charging to the windows of the plant, blasted them with buckshot. The battle was on.

The strikers fought back with every weapon at their disposal. From the roof, from windows, they rained a hail of metal pipes, nuts, bolts, pop bottles, coffee mugs, and two-pound steel automobile door hinges on the heads of the attacking police. For three hours, the battle raged. Throughout, Victor Reuther and the other strike leaders took turns at the microphone on the sound truck, shouting encouragement to their embattled troops, excoriating the police; and when the men in blue tried to charge the truck to silence them, a protective guard of burly unionists beat them back.

Sheriff Thomas Wolcott drove his sedan into the battle zone. Strikers seized it and turned it on its side, its glaring headlights shining on a battlefield littered with broken glass, rocks, and door hinges. Three other police cars were upset. Still the battle raged. Police gathered for one more assault on the door of the plant, but the strikers, armed now with a fire hose, turned a powerful spray of icy water on the attackers, knocking them back. A new barrage of rocks, bottles, and door hinges cascaded down upon their heads, and the men in blue at last broke and ran 50 yards to a bridge that approached the plant gate. Then they ran 50 yards more across it and vanished into the night. Their precipitate retreat led unionists afterwards to dub the clash derisively, "The Battle of the Running Bulls."

It had been, indeed, a battle. Fourteen strikers had been shot and wounded by police gunfire; dozens of others had been beaten, cut, and injured. It was pitched warfare so fierce and so bloody that it spelled a clear message; it warned that even worse violence might be expected. Recognizing the warning, Governor Frank Murphy, who had been elected largely by labor's votes, ordered 1,200 National Guardsmen into Flint. But he made it clear that he sent them to keep order, not to break the strike.

The fierceness of the sit-down warfare placed Murphy in an almost impossible predicament. Labor had helped greatly in his election; he was sympathetic to its demands, and he recognized the arrogance with which General Motors had refused to negotiate with the union. But, at the same time, he recognized that, as governor, it was his duty to uphold the law and protect property rights. The sit-downs certainly violated those rights; they were, in effect, the illegal seizure by labor of the employer's property. This aspect, of course, was all that mattered to big business organizations, to the wealthy, the high placed, and influential. They demanded that the governor act at once to protect property— that he send in the troops and forcibly oust the strikers. But Murphy knew that to do this would cause even greater tragedy, that hundreds of men might be killed. So he temporized and sought a middle course that pleased nobody completely. He kept the National Guardsmen on the scene to maintain order, and he brought pressure on General Motors to sit down at the bargaining table with representatives of the union.

The level-headed course between disastrous extremes seemed at first likely to produce results. Yielding to Murphy's pressure, William Knudsen and GM agreed to meet with the UAW, provided the strikers would leave the plants first. The UAW put no faith in GM's pledge not to operate the plants for 15 days; but under pressure by Murphy, it also yielded. Sit-downers actually left struck GM plants in Detroit and Anderson, Indiana, and they were about to evacuate the Flint plants when Bill Lawrence, a United Press reporter, uncovered an exchange of telegrams that showed Knudsen was planning to meet with Boysen's strike-breaking Flint Alliance. This evidence of what they interpreted as a contemplated double cross so infuriated the

Homer Martin and Walter Reuther, right, helping to lead the victorious sit-downers from a GM plant during a truce

Roy Reuther organizing workers at a Chevrolet plant

Support from the home front for the sit-downers

A red letter day ending the sit-down in Fisher #1

[93]

Flint strikers that they promptly repudiated the agreement and continued to occupy the plants.

Both sides took stock of the situation. The strikers had now been in the seized plants for more than a month, and for GM the situation was becoming desperate. While the shutdown had not been complete, General Motors production had been cut to 1,500 cars a week at a time when Ford was turning out 28,825 and Chrysler 25,350. The economic noose was tightening, and GM was determined to break it. It tried to whip up even greater strength for the back-to-work movement, enlarged the number of guards protecting its remaining plants, and applied to another judge—this time one who didn't hold General Motors stock—for a sweeping, strikebreaking injunction.

This pressure drove the union to countermeasures. As in every battle, there comes a moment when the generals in command must gamble their last shock troops to sweep the board with one bold stroke or lose all. It was such a time now for Robert Travis, the Flint strike leader, and the Reuther brothers, who were his most prominent assistants. They knew that the morale of the men inside the struck plants was weakening. The month-long siege, the lack of outside support, the fading prospect of victory, all were beginning to take their toll. A decisive stroke was needed to enhearten the men and break the back of GM's ability to resist.

In this crisis, Roy Reuther came up with the strategy that the moment demanded. There was in Flint one vital plant that had not been involved in the sit-down. It was Chevrolet Plant No. 4, containing the vital motor assembly division. Among its workers was a hard core of unionists,

[94]

and Roy Reuther proposed that these men, acting in concert with strikers on the outside, should seize the plant. Since a head-on attack would be met by all the GM plant guards and available police, Roy proposed an ingenious strategy.

He and the other strike leaders knew that GM, through its $1,000,000 plant-espionage expenditure, still had active spies within the union. Roy Reuther proposed to make use of them to deceive the opposition and clear the way for the seizure of Plant 4. Travis and the other strike leaders endorsed his strategy and let it be known that the next great objective was to be the seizure of Plant 9, which made only ball bearings. GM and Flint police got the news, as intended, and concentrated forces on protecting Plant 9.

On the afternoon of February 1, the UAW launched its two-pronged action. Inside Plant 9, not one of the strongest union plants, a hard core of workers set up the cry, "Strike! Strike!" Management, alerted by its informers, was prepared for them. Plant guards, Flint detectives, and burly thugs imported especially for the occasion mobbed the strikers, who put up a valiant, desperate battle. Tear gas was hurled by company guards and police. Outside the plant, a women's brigade composed of wives and daughters, specially formed by the UAW and dispatched to the scene, took long poles and smashed plant windows so that their men could get air. A sound truck with a microphone, protected by several hundred strikers, was stationed on the street to lend reality to the scene. For half an hour the battle raged inside and outside Plant 9; then, suddenly, the speaker on the sound truck called on all good unionists to stop fighting and go home. On the instant, the battlers inside and outside the plant obeyed; the disturbance at Plant 9 stopped as if someone had turned off a faucet. For word had arrived that the diversion at Plant 9 had accomplished its purpose; Plant 4 had been captured.

While GM guards and Flint police had been concentrating all their attention on Plant 9, a group of burly "commandos" had been rushed from union headquarters to Plant 4. Aided by a timed uprising inside the plant, they had swept aside astounded company guards, and undeterred by the presence of police, had seized the plant and barricaded its doors and windows. It was without doubt one of the most brilliantly conceived and executed maneuvers of the labor wars of the 1930's and with its success Chevrolet, GM's most popular car and greatest moneymaker, was shut down.

The reaction was one of exultation on the part of the union, of outrage and uncontrolled fury on the part of management and all representatives of the established order. While triumphant strikers gathered on the roofs of their captured plants and shouted the verses of "Solidarity Forever" back and forth at each other, the conservative elements of society almost went berserk. Even Governor Murphy, who had tried to steer a temperate course, became so frustrated and irate that he threatened to have the National Guard drive strikers out of Plant 4 by force if necessary. Food shipments to the men inside both Chevy 4 and Fisher 2 were stopped. The next day, the court issued a new injunction, ordering the strikers to clear out of the seized plants by 3 P.M., February 3, on pain of imprisonment for contempt and the levying of a $15,000,000 fine.

In this pass, Walter Reuther and other UAW leaders turned to John L. Lewis. They urged the redoubtable CIO chieftain to come to Michigan and assume personal command at the strike scene, and Lewis, realizing that the UAW would virtually cease to exist if it failed now, heeded their appeal.

Inside the struck plants, the workers, unable to confer with their leadership, faced with the looming deadline on which their very lives might depend, sat down to consider what they should do. They decided, quite calmly, to stay—and, if need be, to die. In a telegram to Governor Murphy, the workers in Fisher 1 put their case in simple but determined terms. They said, in part:

"Unarmed as we are, the introduction of the militia, sheriffs or police with murderous weapons will mean a blood bath of unarmed workers. . . . We have decided to stay in the plant. We have no illusions about the sacrifices which this decision will entail. We fully expect that if a violent effort is made to oust us many of us will be killed, and we take this means of making it known to our wives, to our children, to the people of the state of Michigan and the country that if this result follows from the attempt to eject us, you are the one who must be held responsible for our deaths."

Murphy received this chilling ultimatum as the day of final decision dawned. In the exclusive Town Club in the Durant Hotel, plant executives, Flint Alliance leaders, and Flint police drank and sang with raucous, mocking accents the strikers' own songs. In the plants, the workers fashioned clubs and blackjacks, using assembly-line methods, and hung these weapons at their waists and waited. Outside, on the roads leading into Flint, a veritable army moved.

It was an army of workers, marching to join their brothers in the struck plants, marching for the showdown. They came with their women, their wives and daughters.

[97]

They came waving placards; they came carrying clubs, sticks, crowbars, stove pokers, clothes trees from which the bases had been knocked off. By battered car, by truck, on foot, they poured into Flint. Walter Reuther led a disciplined phalanx 500 strong from the West Side locals of Detroit. Lansing, Pontiac, and Toledo sent their contingents. Akron's rubber workers, shock troops of the CIO, turned out in strength. As the 3 o'clock deadline for the evacuation of the plants neared, a long cordon of almost 5,000 workers, two abreast, carrying the American flag and brandishing their homemade weapons, circled the lawn that fronted the approach to Fisher 1, singing "Solidarity Forever" as their forebears had sung "Yankee Doodle." And still more volunteers poured in to join the army. Soon all the streets were blocked, and the strikers, from their sound trucks, took over the direction of traffic. Not a policeman was in sight.

The deadline passed. Governor Murphy, a humane man, had no taste for the kind of mass bloodshed that alone could serve management's ends, and so he refrained from issuing the order that would have sent the national guardsmen against the strikers. Instead, in Detroit, he finally prevailed upon Knudsen to meet with Lewis. When the three met, Governor Murphy, suddenly veering, insisted that Lewis order the men to quit the seized plants. Lewis' reply was doughty and blunt: "I do not doubt your ability to call out your soldiers and shoot the members of our union out of those plants," said he, "but let me say when you issue that order I shall leave this conference and I shall enter one of those plants with my people."

Murphy had to retreat. He wired Sheriff Wolcott to take no action against the strikers. Boysen and the General

Motors' attorneys raged at the Governor and the Sheriff, but the union legions massed around the plants went wild with joy. The sit-down strikers' band in Fisher 1 played hillbilly airs, men and women square danced on the hard-frozen lawns, wives passed children through the windows to their husbands, and above all the voices of the faithful rose in the roared anthem, "Solidarity Forever," one of whose stanzas seemed especially apt. It goes:

"In our hands is placed a power greater than their hoarded gold,
"Greater than the might of atoms and magnified a thousand-fold;
"We can bring to birth a new world from the ashes of the old
"For the union makes us strong"

Days of delicate negotiations still lay ahead, but on February 11, 1937, the end came. General Motors signed a contract giving the UAW exclusive bargaining rights in its plants. The auto firm agreed that no workers would be punished for strike activity, all would be rehired; it agreed to drop the injunction and contempt proceedings against the Flint sit-downers; it permitted workers to wear their union buttons and to discuss the union with fellow workers at lunch and rest periods, basic American freedoms that had previously been denied; and it granted a five-cents-an-hour wage increase. It was a tremendous victory, one that literally made the UAW and the CIO going and powerful concerns. Workers rushed to join the victorious union, and in a few weeks UAW membership doubled from 100,000 to 200,000.

In the first flush of triumph, sit-downs broke out everywhere. The height of the wave came in March 1937, when 192,642 workers squatted at their jobs. The bulk of these, some 60,000 of them, were in Chrysler plants. This second of the Big Three auto giants held out for four weeks, but then it, too, was forced to yield and recognize the union. Studebaker and Cadillac also signed up, and there was left in the entire auto industry just one titan who still defied the UAW —the great Ford Motor Company.

Walter Reuther, who had worked long years for Ford, knew firsthand the brutality and the strength of the Ford dictatorship. No gentler words serve to describe it. For Henry Ford, in his iron determination that no union should ever get a foothold inside the gates of a Ford plant, had taken a onetime Navy pugilist, Harry Bennett, and made him, under Ford himself, the virtual czar of the Ford empire. He had risen with Ford's blessing from the post of head watchman at the Rouge plant to the command of the Ford Service Department, the army of some 3,000 pugs, thugs, and gangsters whom Ford used to terrorize his workers and keep them in subjection.

Keith Sward, a sober and careful writer, subsequently composed this description of what conditions were like in Ford plants under Bennett:

"For years after Bennett came to power, it was the proud, undisguised aim of the Service Department to blot out every manifestation of personality or manliness inside a Ford plant. . . . Bennett's mercenaries finally mastered every tactic from the swagger of the Prussian drill sergeant to outright sadism and physical assault. On the night shift they would jolt an incoming worker out of his wits and take the starch out of his system by flashing a light in his face and shouting at him, 'Where did you get that badge?' or 'Who's your boss?' Another intimidating practice that came into being under Bennett's rule was the act of 'shaking 'em up in the aisles.' In this case a workman summoned to the employment office for any reason at all, even one that was totally unrelated to his work, would be shoved and pushed along the aisle by a pair of officious Servicemen, like a felon in the custody of police."

Among the Servicemen were such as "Legs" Laman, rumrunner, kidnapper, and squealer who after six years in prison was paroled in the custody of Ford; Chester LaMare, a powerful Detroit gang leader who was rewarded for his allegiance with the fruit and vegetable concession at River Rouge, worth $100,000 a year; Sam Cuva, who had been jailed for the indiscretion of shooting his mother-in-law; Angelo Caruso, leader of the Detroit Down River gang; and such professional wrestlers as Sarkisian and Ted Greis. These were the kind of musclemen whom Walter Reuther decided to challenge in the spring of 1937 in the attempt to organize Ford. Henry Ford had announced that he would never recognize the UAW or any other union, and he meant it. Forewarned by the fate that had befallen General Motors and Chrysler, he strengthened Bennett's goon squad and stepped up the campaign by espionage and terrorism in the plants. Some workers secretly joined the UAW, but they risked their jobs in doing so. The first faint whiff of suspicion coming to the nostrils of one of Bennett's hirelings was sufficient to bounce them into the street among the still plentiful millions of unemployed.

The kind of acts that merited discharge are indicative of the challenge the UAW faced in its attempt to organize Ford. One worker had concealed some union application cards in his cap. When he took his cap off to wipe perspiration from his forehead, the cards fluttered out, were spotted by one of Bennett's spies—and the man was fired. Another, who liked to play baseball, happened one day to play on a union ball team, though he was not a member of the union. Two of Bennett's stooges spotted him, and he was fired. Still another worker saw a newspaper article quoting Henry Ford as saying he guessed he couldn't do much about unions now since the U.S. Supreme Court had upheld the Wagner Labor Relations Act. The worker suggested to his foreman that perhaps he should read the article—and was promptly fired. But probably no story of capricious firing at Ford matches the experience of a worker named John Gallo. One day, while working on the assembly line, Gallo happened to smile. A Bennett stool pigeon caught him in the act—and Gallo was fired.

Walter Reuther decided that it was hopeless, with Bennett's spies lurking on every assembly line, to try to organize Ford secretly. The Supreme Court had upheld the legality of the Wagner Act; unions had a *right* to organize, guaranteed to them by the highest court in the land; and the thing to do was to move openly against Ford, wrapped in this mantle of legal protection. The first move would be the distribution of union handbills at the gates of Ford's River Rouge plant at shift-changing time on the afternoon of May 26, 1937.

There was to be no secrecy about the endeavor. Dearborn had passed a law banning the distribution of such literature without a permit. Reuther applied for and obtained a permit. Some 60 loyal unionists, two-thirds of them women, agreed to attempt the risky feat of testing Henry Ford's respect for the law. Reuther himself was to lead the

[102]

delegation, backed up by Richard Frankensteen, a UAW vice-president, and Richard Merriweather and Ralph Dunham, auto workers.

It was a cloudy afternoon when Walter Reuther, Frankensteen, Merriweather, and Dunham, carrying their handbills, left a streetcar and mounted the long flights of iron steps leading to an overpass outside the River Rouge plant. As they reached the overpass, they encountered a delegation of newspaper reporters and photographers from all of the Detroit papers, the Associated Press, the New York *Times*, *Time* magazine, and other publications. The photographers asked Reuther and his aides to pause a moment for pictures. They did. Then they turned toward the plant gates.

In that moment, a prize selection of Harry Bennett's toughest toughs appeared. A photographer caught this scene: Walter Reuther, neatly dressed as usual, watch chain gleaming across his vest, advanced toward the plant gates, handbills under his arm, a smile upon his face. Advancing upon him and his aides came the grimly glowering swarm of Bennett's thugs. The contrast between smiles and menace foretold what was about to happen.

Walter Reuther later described the events of the next few minutes in sworn testimony before the National Labor Relations Board, and his version was corroborated by the independent testimony of six newsmen who were present.

"After the pictures were taken, we were approached by men from all sides. One called out that we were on private property and to get the hell out of there. Frankensteen and I started to walk towards the north stairway to get off the bridge in obedience to the command. I had hardly taken three steps when I was slugged on the back of the head. I tried to shield my face by crossing my arms. They pounded me all over the head and body. . . . I was knocked to the ground and beaten. The leader said, 'That's enough, fellows.' I thought I was released. But they picked me up and threw me down bodily on the concrete floor of the platform. Then they kicked me again and again. They tried to tear my legs apart.

"Seven times they raised me off the concrete and threw me down on it. They pinned my arms and shot short jabs to my face. I was punched and dragged by my feet to the stairway. I grabbed the railing and they wrenched me loose. I was thrown down the first flight of iron steps. Then they kicked me down the other two flights of stairs until I found myself on the ground, where I was beaten and kicked. . . . At about this time girls and women who came from Detroit with circulars tried to get off the streetcars, and so the men seemed to lose interest in me."

Frankensteen was similarly mauled. A news photograph showed his coat and vest being whipped up over his head, imprisoning his arms while his body was being beaten by his attackers. Dunham was caught and brutally beaten several blocks from the overpass. He was so badly injured that he was confined to a hospital for ten days, during which time he suffered from constant internal bleeding. Merriweather's back was broken, and when he testified before the National Labor Relations Board, he was still in a cast. Tony Marinovich, another union man who arrived on the streetcar with the handbill-carrying women, was beaten so brutally that physicians predicted he would never walk again.

While Walter Reuther and Frankensteen lay in bruised and battered heaps at the foot of the stairs down which they had been thrown and kicked, Bennett's men turned on the group of women descending from the streetcar. The men beat them, knocked them down, trampled them, kicked them in the stomach. Bennett's men then turned upon the newspaper men, mauled them, and grabbed and smashed cameras, destroying their films. During all the time that these brutalities, which became known as "The Battle of Overpass," were being committed in the name of Ford and anti-unionism, a delegation of Dearborn police stood idly by.

"The Battle of the Overpass" created a momentary shock wave from coast to coast. It showed in graphic, undeniable fashion the kind of rule that the men in the auto plants had had to buck, the ruthlessness that had made both unionism and sit-downs necessary. Ford, of course, could not be expected to recognize such fundamental truths, and when *Time* printed a devastating account of the affair, the Ford Company penalized the magazine by withdrawing its advertising for nearly a year and a half.

While these repercussions were developing, while Walter Reuther was recovering from his lumps and bruises and his more seriously injured union helpers lay in agony in the hospitals, John L. Lewis sent them all a chins-up wire. "Keep your poise," it read. "It is merely an instance." The words must have seemed totally inadequate to men with internal injuries or a broken back, but in the larger sense Lewis was a prophet. "The Battle of the Overpass" was, indeed, "merely an instance"—an instance that marked the beginning of the downfall of Ford's anti-unionism.

For some three months later, Walter Reuther was back in front of the gates of the River Rouge plant, distributing handbills. This time he came escorted. A thousand muscular

JAMES KILPATRICK: THE DETROIT NEWS

The attack on Frankensteen
during the Battle of the Overpass

unionists stood around, just to make certain that the one-sided "Battle of the Overpass" was not repeated, and Bennett's men, noting their number and their muscles, stayed within the confines of the plant.

Walter Reuther had become by now the most hated man in Detroit, perhaps in all the country, among the conservative employer-manager-business classes. He was the recognized architect of the sit-down, the mastermind of the Kelsey-Hayes strike, the man who had furnished much of the brains and muscle that had beaten General Motors. Now he was a threat to Ford, and because he was, somebody evidently decided that he would have to go.

On the night of April 9, 1938, a group of friends and relatives were celebrating Sophie Reuther's birthday in the La Salle Boulevard apartment. In the midst of the jollification came a knock at the door. Walter, who has had a fondness for Chinese food ever since his world tour, had ordered chop suey sent over from a neighborhood restaurant, and he assumed that the knock heralded the arrival of the chop-suey bearers. He was wrong.

The door crashed open, and two men entered, one flourishing a blackjack, the other a gun. The man with the gun pointed it at Walter. "Come on. We want you."

Many men, staring into the muzzle of death and hoping to prolong the event, might have gone quietly. But not Walter. He leaped back into a corner, grabbed a floor lamp, and prepared to lay about him. Sophie grabbed and threw a pickle jar. In an instant, all was bedlam. One of the guests, Al King, edged toward the kitchen, threw up a window, and leaped two floors to the ground, narrowly missing a concrete incinerator. Miraculously landing in one piece, he set off down the street, yelling for the police at the top of his lungs. Back in the living room of the apartment, Walter had swatted at the blackjack-carrier with the floor lamp, then had closed and grappled with him in a wrestler's clutch. Walter's athletic years and the fact that he had never let himself get out of condition now came in handy. He wrenched the blackjack out of the thug's hand and flipped it to his brother Roy, who, he figured, might have an opportunity to put it to good use on the skull of the gunman. This one, now sought a simple solution.

"Let's just plug him here," he growled to his comrade.

"If you do, you'll never get out alive," Roy told him, brandishing the blackjack.

King's shouts by now were raising a hubbub on the street, and a crowd was gathering below. Preferring to save their own skins, the intruders abandoned their bungled mission and fled. A few days later, Walter got a mysterious telephone call from an informer, who assured Walter he could give him the names of the two party-crashing thugs for a price—$5,000. All Walter had to do to get the names was to meet the informer in a bar with the money.

Recognizing that the whole thing might be a trap to accomplish what had been bungled the first time, Walter decided, nevertheless, that it was worth the gamble. It was quite a decision for him to make in more ways than one, for Walter doesn't drink or smoke. "It was probably the first time," a friend says, "that Walter had ever been in a dive." He did not go alone. At the appointed hour, the bar was fairly crawling with strong-muscled UAW members, sipping their beers and keeping their eyes on Walter. The informant, not suspecting, showed up and was quickly surrounded.

He turned out to have surprisingly solid information. The two men he named were a pair of Harry Bennett's "Servicemen." They were identified, arrested, and, in essence, admitted all. But when they were brought to trial, they gave a new twist to the story. They insisted that Walter himself had hired them to jump him. His purpose? Publicity. This preposterous story won the pair a jury acquittal.

Some years later, in 1941, after Ford had bowed to the UAW and signed a contract, one of the men telephoned a UAW official with a novel proposition. He thought it would be nice, he said, if he and the UAW official could arrange to have Walter and Bennett meet at dinner. The suggestion so outraged the UAW aide that he let forth with a volley of unprintable language. The caller, who evidently considered himself a businessman who had been hired to do a job—and it did not matter, of course, that the job was a little thing like murder—was quite offended. "You guys didn't take that personally, did you?" he asked.

The odd part of it is that Walter didn't. He has a strangely objective attitude regarding himself. He recognized that, in the kind of no-holds-barred fight he was waging, he inevitably made enemies, extremely powerful enemies; and he realized that, when the stakes are so high, when so much power and prestige is at stake, a lot of men will do almost anything to win. It was to him a simple fact of life, and so, after the Chop-Suey Incident, as it became known to the Reuthers, he applied for a gun permit and began carrying a revolver everywhere he went. He had a hunch that his life was still in danger; and, as events were to show a few years later, he was right.

Chapter 8

Man of Controversy

Success made Walter Reuther one of the most controversial men in America, a distinction he still retains. Within a few years, he vaulted from obscurity into headline prominence as one of the most powerful labor leaders in the nation. He was in the van of the swirling actions that shocked and alarmed many people. His name became inseparably linked with the sit-down strike, with the wild turbulence of the General Motors showdown, and the "Battle of the Overpass" at Ford; and many Americans felt an almost instinctive distrust of such a stormy petrel. That attitude, to some degree, still persists.

Big business, of course, did its utmost to foster this distrust. The multimillionaire motor barons of Detroit, men whose will had been law for decades, could not brook the idea that now they must share their power with a union, and they could not abide the person who had been the principal creator of this state of affairs. Their venom knew no bounds. Beginning early and continuing for more than a quarter of a century, they conducted a persistent propaganda campaign to paint Reuther as a Communist, a bloody Bolshevik, at the very least a dangerous, red-tainted radical. George Romney, of American Motors, later Republican Governor of Michigan, once called Reuther "the most dangerous man in Detroit, because no one is more skilful at bringing about revolution without seeming to disturb the existing order of society." Other business spokesmen have intimated that Reuther wants to run for President; they picture him as a man whose ruthless ambition knows no bounds; they draw frightening images of him as a labor czar in the White House and suggest that, in this event, he would become the first American dictator. Most of these fantasies are too wild for credence, but there is no question that they have served their purpose—to instil doubts about Reuther in the minds of a large percentage of the American electorate.

The birth of such doubts may be traced back to the wild winter of 1936-37 when the epidemic of sit-down strikes and the outburst of widespread violence frightened many Americans with the spectre of revolution. The business classes and conservatives of every stripe were naturally startled, outraged, and apprehensive. They were not alone. The great American middle class, traditionally the backbone of our society, reacted perhaps less violently, but still with deep disturbance and distrust. Having a strong sense of the sacredness of private property and the free enterprise system, and viewing the spectacle of sit-down strikers usurping the plants of their employers and using them as a battleground, many middle-of-the-road Americans, just as did the wealthy and conservative classes, looked on Walter Reuther's "industrial revolution" as close to a real revolution—a violent, bloody, dangerous upheaval of the masses.

The furore in Congress that the sit-downs touched off mirrored these deep concerns. Republicans, Southern Democrats, and even some of the more moderate legislators viewed with horror and alarm, and these viewings were prominently displayed in a predominantly conservative press. Senator Hiram Johnson (Rep., California) warned that the sit-downs would lead to dictatorship; Senator J. Ham Lewis (Dem., Illinois) thundered that the rights of private property were endangered; Senator William King (Dem., Utah) denounced the sit-downs as a CIO technique for bolshevizing the nation; Senators Arthur Vandenberg (Rep., Michigan) and Millard Tydings (Dem., Maryland) assailed both the sit-downs and the Wagner Act, which had made labor powerful. There were demands for investigations, for laws to prohibit sit-downs, for action to change the Wagner Act and to impose curbs on labor.

Liberal senators, some of whom had sincere doubts themselves about the legality of the sit-downs, were in the minority and had difficulty making themselves heard in this overwhelming chorus. Nevertheless, they put up a spirited defense. The most forceful and most eloquent speech in defense of the sitdowns was made by Senator Robert Wagner (Dem., New York), the author of the Wagner Act. He declared the strikes had been provoked "by longstanding ruthless tactics of a few great corporations who have hamstrung the National Labor Relations Board . . . who have openly banded together to defy this law of Congress . . . and who have systematically used spies and discharges and violence and terrorism to shatter the workers' liberties as de-

[113]

fined by Congress. . . . The organized and calculated and cold-blooded sit-down against Federal law has come, as always not from the common people, but from a few great vested interests."

In the end the Senate passed by a vote of 75 to 3 a resolution that said in effect "a plague on both your houses." On the one hand, it denounced the sit-downs as "illegal and contrary to public policy"; on the other, it declared that industrial espionage, the denial by employers of the right of collective bargaining, and the fostering of company unions were also contrary to sound public policy. The view that the sit-downs had been an illegal device was later upheld by the U.S. Supreme Court.

By the time the Supreme Court acted, however, the issue had become academic, for labor itself had virtually abandoned the device. The wave of sit-downs, which had reached a peak in March 1937, quickly tapered off after the Supreme Court upheld the Wagner Act. In the face of this ruling, most employers agreed to bargain collectively with unions, and both the need for sit-downs and their employment by labor as a strike weapon swiftly passed.

Only a few months time was needed to change the entire outlook of the nation and to expose the earlier wild fears for the false alarm that they had been. There was no revolution. There was no continuing struggle and bloodshed. The entire economy was not "bolshevized," but on the contrary management and labor discovered that it was quite possible to sit down and negotiate fair contracts. Working conditions and the wages of labor steadily improved, and this development, far from ruining business, created a healthier climate of public opinion in which business itself could prosper. The result, it might seem, should have done much to dispel the idea that Walter Reuther was a dangerous, wild-swinging radical intent on the complete subversion of the American system, but it did not. For once a man has been branded an extremist, has been in the forefront of violent action, the public frequently remain either scared or hostile.

In Reuther's case, too, lending color to the charges, there was the indisputable fact of Socialist connections. Walter had not only taken to the stump for Norman Thomas in 1932, but he remained for years a Socialist. In the election of 1937, with the sit-downs and the "Battle of the Overpass" fresh in everyone's mind, he ran on the Socialist ticket for councilman in Detroit. He polled 126,160 votes, but he finished fifteenth in the list of candidates, badly beaten. The outcome vividly demonstrated the distaste of most Americans for radical or third-party ties. When a man as well-known as Reuther, with heavy labor following as a nucleus of support, could not do any better than this, the handwriting was clearly on the wall for the demise of the Socialist Party.

Walter Reuther has always been a man with a passion for facts, and he recognized the signs clearly. This recognition led the following year to his break with Socialism. In 1938, there was a hot gubernatorial campaign in Michigan. Governor Frank Murphy, whose humaneness and sympathy for labor had resulted in the avoidance of wholesale bloodshed in the Flint General Motors strike, was the Democratic candidate to succeed himself. Reuther, the "pragmatic idealist," felt that it was imperative for labor to support the reelection of Murphy. The Socialist Party insisted on run-

[115]

ning its own candidate, but Reuther saw that such a campaign, if at all successful, could serve only to split the liberal vote and propel into office the type of governor labor would not want. He made it known, therefore, that he was backing Murphy and offered to resign from the Socialist Party. Though Norman Thomas himself appealed to him not to resign before the election and though Reuther honored this appeal, his break with the party was definite, and the formal severing of relations came soon afterwards. Reuther's choice was one that many American liberals were making in those years. Since the Republican Party was primarily the party of opposition and the defender of the status quo, "pragmatic idealists" like Reuther sought haven with the Democrats.

That Reuther became and remained a Democrat naturally has not appeased his critics. To them, he remains the same old "radical" Socialist, as dangerous as ever, perhaps even more so now that he is "disguised" as a Democrat. To arch-conservatives, unable or unwilling to distinguish between Socialism and Communism or to recognize that such Socialists as Norman Thomas are Communism's bitterest enemies, Reuther remains a "bloody Bolshevik" and the great menace of our times. The record, like the whole personality of Reuther himself, gives the lie to such canards.

Louis Budenz, prominent Communist Party leader, told after his break with Communism how the party made a determined effort in 1935-37 to woo Reuther and other Socialists believed to be sympathetic to Russia into accepting party membership. Reuther, according to Budenz and others, balked when he was told that he would have to submit to the iron discipline of the party, especially on foreign affairs, and spurned the offer. This evidence that Reuther was never a Communist does not mollify his critics. They retort that he worked for years hand-in-glove with Communists in the labor movement. This is true to the extent that the interests of some of the Communist and pro-Communist labor leaders sometimes coincided with his. When this happened, the two joined forces; but the record of the turbulent 1940's that witnessed Reuther's steady climb to power shows clearly that such alliances were always accidental and temporary. Reuther, on major issues, constantly collided with the Communist Party line and was vilified repeatedly by Communist Party organs.

The picture becomes clear only if one traces the complex, unceasing war that raged within the UAW. The internal battle for power burst into flame almost in the first flush of victory. Hardly had the UAW won its titanic struggle with General Motors and begun to enroll the auto workers by the tens of thousands when its own structure began to creak and groan from the stress of its own birth pains. The battle focused on and raged about President Homer Martin.

The onetime preacher had been a valuable front man for the union in the days of its hard, early struggles. Then the problem had been to arouse the workers and whip them up to the point where they would dare to take the risky step of joining a union, where they would dare to tackle management. Martin's rich, pulpit-style oratory had been ideally suited to the needs of the moment, to the leadership of a holy crusade; but once that crusade resulted in victory, the problem became an administrative one—how to handle and organize the fruits of victory—and, at that point, Homer Martin was lost. He quickly demonstrated that he was a bumbling administrator; and, unfortunately, like many bumblers, he had an exaggerated opinion of his own abilities. It was a fatal combination, especially in circumstances that required a deft and skilful touch.

The UAW's great victory over General Motors was not an imperishable and indestructible monument like the pyramids. It was a triumph that needed careful tending, lest suddenly it melt away. Problems thronged in its wake. The victorious unionists acted for a time as if they owned the world; they carried, as one union writer has put it, "not a chip but a log upon their shoulders." General Motors, on the other hand, showed a tendency to forget that the Battle of Flint had ever happened, much less that it had been lost, and for quite a spell, it persisted in trying by every device to nibble away at the union's power. Both sides were wrong, and the collisions between them were frequent. And the workers, finding that the corporation often still refused to give a hearing to what they considered just grievances, resorted to a series of brief work stoppages, "wildcat" strikes.

Martin, trying to live up to his conception of the role of responsible labor leader, denounced such demonstrations and, in one letter, practically joined the ranks of management by conceding that GM had the right to fire such demonstrators. It goes almost without saying that a union leader who does not stand up for his men loses his following. There was great discontent in the union over Martin's stand, and Walter Reuther, recognizing this, adopted a position that was much more in tune with the mood of the workers when he wrote: "It looks very much as though General Motors does not want an agreement with the UAW. Now let's see what it would mean if the union decided to call off negotiations. The workers would then be free to demand a lot of conditions and wages that are due them, and they could sit down every time these were denied. . . . There would be a lot of strikes if there were no agreement."

The dispute between Martin and his once faithful followers came to a head at the UAW convention in Milwaukee in August 1937. In addition to the dispute over Martin's stand on wildcat strikes, the union president had drafted proposed changes in the UAW constitution that would have given him greatly increased, if not dictatorial, powers. This last move, coupled with the underlying discontent, touched off one of those name-calling, free-for-all convention floor battles for which the UAW was to become famous.

Martin, finding himself stoutly opposed, lashed out viciously. He fired several organizers, Roy and Victor Reuther among them, and tarred his critics with the charge that "an outside organization" (he meant, of course, the Communist Party) was trying to seize control of the union. Unfortunately for Martin, his own inner circle of advisers included a number of Communists who had been ousted from the party in a factional fight, and so it was quite a delicate question which combination in the present struggle was more "outside" than the other.

There is no doubt that the anti-Martin coalition, in which the Reuthers were central figures, received powerful and important help from Communists within the union. In numerical following, the strongest leader of the coalition was Wyndham Mortimer, and the well organized Communist core within the union supported and strengthened the coalition. Nevertheless, Martin could not go red-baiting with entirely clean hands himself, and his tactics rubbed many of the delegates on a particularly tender and sensitive spot.

"Communist" was not the dirty word it later became. Communists were looked upon as domestic radicals, not too much different from other radicals, and it was to be several years before it was generally recognized that they were the stooges of Moscow, puppets to be jerked on the Russian string. Furthermore, in the early days of the labor movement, many of the best organizers were Communists, for the simple reason that up to that time only the Communists had been idealistic enough or fanatical enough to pay any great attention to union agitation and organization. All UAW men knew this, and they knew, too, that a favorite tactic of employers was to brand *all* labor leaders "Reds" and to imply that the striking rank and file were either of the same deep dye or weak-minded, addled dupes. Understandably, union men did not take kindly to such all-inclusive labeling, nor did they look with favor upon men who indulged in it.

The result was that, in a convention that several times verged on fisticuffs, John L. Lewis himself had to exercise his authority in the role of peacemaker. A compromise was arranged, and Martin emerged from the fracas still in control of the union, with a majority of the executive board in his hip pocket, but with stature and prestige among the rank and file much diminished. Martin now embarked upon an insane and suicidal course. Drunk with power, he developed a mania for firing his closest aids. In June 1938, he lopped off five high official heads, including those of Addes, Mortimer, and Frankensteen. When a rank-and-file delegation tried to protest some of his arbitrary acts, Martin confronted its members with a revolver. Other rank and filers were even less fortunate. They found that they couldn't even get to see their president.

All the time, it seems, it should have been perfectly possible for Martin, by a more rational course of action, to have formed an alliance with the strongest supporter he could have had. For Walter Reuther, too, was having his troubles. The strongly organized Communist bloc in the union was after his scalp. In November 1937, the Communists tried to split his strong West Side local into several smaller ones. Failing in this, they used all their influence in the Michigan CIO convention in April 1938, to defeat Victor Reuther for a high union post. It should have been quite obvious to Martin that the Reuthers stood alone and needed allies, even as he needed allies. But Martin could not see this. He persisted in antagonizing the only man of power in the UAW who might have helped him.

Arrogantly, he supplanted Walter Reuther in the handling of the attempt to organize Ford. He plainly implied that Walter had bungled the job and that the only way to see it was done right was for him, Martin, to take charge himself. Martin's conception of the way to deal with Ford, however, was fantastic. He developed the notion that Henry Ford was a kindly old man who didn't really know what was happening in his plants. All that was needed was to sit down with him, talk with him, open his eyes—and all would be well. Ford promptly threw cold water on his idealistic conception of himself by refusing to have anything to do with Martin. Even so, Martin wasn't discouraged. There was kindly Harry Bennett, the boss of the 3,000 "gentlemen" in Ford's Service Department; *he* was only too happy to discuss a deal with Homer Martin. The exact nature of the deal that Bennett and Martin discussed has always remained a matter of great controversy, but the odor of such secret dealings was rank in the nostrils of union men. In January 1939, the stench became even worse when R. J. Thomas, one of Martin's principal lieutenants, broke with him. Thomas charged he had been present at conferences at which Martin and a Ford official had discussed devious ways of taking the UAW out of the CIO.

Credence was lent to the charge by the fact that the parent CIO, alarmed by Martin's erratic behavior, had already found it necessary to strip him of some of his powers and place the union in a temporary receivership. This affront was not easily swallowed by Martin, and in March 1939, he confirmed the suspicions of his critics by leading his personal followers out of the UAW and setting up a splinter union, which he promptly affiliated with the A. F. of L. There his group, lacking any real support among the automobile workers of Detroit, quickly became a nuisance outfit of value to no one except the employers.

The departure of Martin from the UAW left the Communists as the best organized force in the union. While they did not by any means represent the bulk of the workers, they were in highly placed, strategic positions, an ideal spot to take over. Walter Reuther, at the head of his 32,000-man West Side local, and R. J. Thomas, leading some middle-of-the-road unionists, represented their most formidable opposition. But it was highly questionable whether Reuther and Thomas could prevail; and the parent CIO, alarmed at the possibility of a Communistic takeover of one of its strongest unions, sent Philip Murray and Sidney Hillman to the UAW's Cleveland convention. There Murray and Hillman faced down the Communist plotters and secured the selection of Thomas as a "compromise" candidate."

All of this internal bickering was as appetizing as a seven-course dinner for the motor magnates. With the UAW seemingly torn apart by internal feuds, they developed the not unreasonable idea that the union was no longer a menace; and in the spring of 1939, General Motors announced it was suspending all collective bargaining. In a clever tactical move to muddy the waters, General Motors also applied to the National Labor Relations Board for an election to see whether the UAW or Homer Martin's new paper A. F. of L. union really represented its workers. It was obvious that a new showdown with GM was inevitable, and in this crisis it was Walter Reuther who came forward with the strategy that led to victory.

Walter, from his long experience in auto plants, appreciated the key role played by tool and die makers. They were the vital men, the indispensable men, during this summer of 1939 when, he knew, GM would be retooling for its new 1940 models. A strike by the tool and die makers at this sensitive time would halt all work on the new models and put GM at a serious disadvantage with its competitors. At the same time, the far more numerous workers on the production lines would not be affected. They could go on working and drawing pay, or, if GM laid them off, they would become immediately eligible for unemployment insurance.

The wiliness of the plan is obvious. On July 6, 1939, Reuther pulled 800 key tool and die workers off the job in 12 struck GM plants. General Motors kept the production lines going for two weeks, then laid off the workers who, as Reuther had foreseen, at once began drawing unemployment compensation. The strike, tough and violent, raged on. There

[123]

were physical clashes at GM plants in Detroit and Cleveland as the corporation strove to break out of the bind in which Reuther had placed it. All its efforts were futile. Without the tool and die makers, all retooling for the new models was stopped, and General Motors was helpless in a competitive market. Finally, in August, the corporation surrendered and signed an agreement giving the UAW exclusive bargaining rights in all its 42 plants, the first such corporation-wide agreement it had ever signed. This second great triumph over General Motors spurred other conquests. A strike at Chrysler was won, and the UAW, freed of the burden of Homer Martin, turned once more to unionizing Ford.

Despite the "Battle of the Overpass" and the Chop Suey Incident, despite Walter Reuther's success in distributing union leaflets at the gates of River Rouge, Harry Bennett's strong-arm men had kept Ford an open-shop citadel that defied the attacks of labor. But the twentieth century, slowly and belatedly, was inexorably catching up with even Henry Ford.

A key force in the process was a series of court decisions upholding the rights of labor. Bennett's gangsterlike tactics might cow the workers inside the Ford plants for a time, but these tactics began to lose their effect when the National Labor Relations Board ruled that between 1936 and 1941 Ford had discharged 2,566 workers illegally for union membership—and that these men must be reinstated in their jobs and paid back pay amounting to $2,000,000! Ford fought every ruling, carrying its legal actions all the way to the U.S. Supreme Court, but Ford lost. Its repeated defeats began to speak more loudly to the workers than even the Bennett terror.

By 1941 the CIO and the UAW had determined to score a breakthrough at Ford. Together, they gathered a large strike fund. Every union in Detroit helped in contacting and propagandizing Ford workers. Membership in the Ford plants soared. As it did, the seething tensions on the assembly line, so long repressed, mounted to a feverish, explosive pitch. Men who had been treated like animals for years hungered to get even. Ford, sensing the growing trouble, seemed for a time about to compromise, but the appearance was deceptive. Compromise was foreign to Harry Bennett. On April 1, 1941, he arrogantly announced that Ford would refuse to meet with any union committees, and he fired eight workers from the grievance committee of Local 600. That did it. The men in the Ford plants quit their jobs and announced they wouldn't go back until the discharged committeemen had been rehired. In the rolling mill plant, where 6,000 workers quit as one man, tempers flared when 110 Dearborn police came charging to the aid of Ford. But thousands of other workers began to march on the rolling mill to help their fellows, and the Dearborn police hastily withdrew.

The strike, so spontaneously called, caught the UAW leadership unaware. Union officials had been building toward a strike, but they had not contemplated action yet. By acting when they did, the rank and file had taken the decision out of their officers' hands. At first union officials couldn't believe it; at first, all Detroit couldn't believe it. The word spread like a sheet of flame, incredible but true—Ford was shut down! Meeting hastily, the union leadership took the only action it could. At 12:15 A.M. on April 2, it ordered the strike against Ford.

In the plants the striking workers greeted the news with shouts of joy; they formed a parade and marched to the union hall a mile away. There an all-night session mapped strike plans. The meeting was chaired by Emil Mazey, a union leader at Briggs and one of Walter Reuther's strongest supporters; and Reuther, Addes, Thomas, virtually every UAW leader of prominence, spoke to the excited men. Mazey afterwards recalled that night as "among the most exciting in our whole experience in the labor movement. It was like seeing men who had been half dead suddenly come to life. And did they come to life! It was hard to keep things going, hard to organize, so eager were they just to mill around and talk and let some steam go. That night you really understood what the union could mean to men."

With the dawn came the crucial test. Inside Ford, Harry Bennett and his men were ready. Outside, the unionists laid their plans. The Ford plant was like an island surrounded by a sea of converging roads. The strikers established barricades of automobiles at some distance from the plant, blocking off every incoming road at a key intersection. Not knowing this, Bennett's men prepared to smash the picket lines to let strikebreakers through as the hour of 6 A.M. approached. But the hour came and passed, and no strikebreakers appeared. The roadblocks had worked.

Enraged and frustrated, Bennett launched an assault on the UAW-CIO picket line an hour later. A barrage of iron bolts and nuts was hurled from the roof of the factory as a column of several hundred, mostly Negroes, armed with steel bars and knives, charged the pickets. In the melee, 36 unionists were injured so badly they had to be hospitalized, and the picket lines were temporarily broken. Thousands more workers rushed to the embattled front, reestablished their cordon about the plant, and at 9 A.M., when Bennett's toughs rushed again, they were beaten back with baseball bats, fists, and clubs. Through it all, the Dearborn police stood idly by, as they had at the "Battle of the Overpass," and only the strength of the union battalions, marshalled in overwhelming numbers, kept Bennett's army in check.

The strike raged on, fierce and bitter. Ford pulled Homer Martin out of its conspiratorial hat, and the onetime president of the UAW completed the act of suicide by urging Detroit's Negroes to "march back in a body" to break the strike called by the union he once had headed. No one loves a turncoat, and with this act Martin completed his own ruin. Nobody was listening to him any more, and even the A. F. of L. repudiated him as a strikebreaker.

It was obvious now that Ford could not break the strike. It would have to settle. Gov. Murray D. Van Wagoner of Michigan proposed terms that were not all the UAW wanted, but that were still acceptable. The union agreed to take them, and so, on April 10, did Ford. In a subsequent NLRB election, the UAW polled 50,000 of the 80,000 votes cast.

Harry Bennett, in a reaction typical of the man and the kind of management mentality he represented, commented sourly: "It's a great victory for the Communist Party, Governor Van Wagoner, and the National Labor Relations Board." Communism, of course, had had nothing to do with the strike or the victory.

Fortunately, Bennett, with defeat, became no longer the sole voice of power at Ford. Henry Ford himself decided that the time had come to end the long reign of his muscleman, and so he sat down with Philip Murray and negotiated a contract that amazed the UAW by its liberal terms. It was one of the most startling about-faces in American labor history; but Ford, having been beaten, having decided that he was going to have to live with the union, evidently determined that he was going to make the living as pleasant as possible.

The contract he signed granted wage increases up to 30 cents an hour, making Ford rates once again the highest in the industry; it abolished Bennett's goon squad; it accepted the union shop, dues checkoff, grievance machinery, the principle of seniority in hiring; it agreed to the reinstatment of workers previously fired for union affiliations; it granted time-and-a-half for overtime, double time for Sundays, two hours pay for workers called to the plant but then not given work. It was the best contract in the automobile field, and within a year it put an additional $52,000,000 into the pockets of Ford employees. The war that Walter Reuther had launched in the "Battle of the Overpass" had been resoundingly won.

Chapter 9

Dynamo of the UAW

F riends and foes, close union aides, and management's masters of executive row never cease to be amazed by Walter Reuther. The amazement began early, grew as his power grew in the Ford and General Motors strikes, and today endures as a state of shocked incredulity. It is no wonder, for Reuther resembles a human dynamo.

The energy of the man is so boundless that lesser men sometimes become exhausted in the mere contemplation of it. Working 12 to 18 hours a day is routine for Walter. He gets drunk on ideas the way some men do on wine, and wherever he goes, he is always cramming statistical reports into a bulging briefcase so that no moment in car or plane may be lost. His mind wades voraciously through jungles of facts and figures, but he never seems to get lost. He always seems to know where he's going and how to get there.

Emil Mazey, one of the younger and more brilliant UAW leaders who was drawn into Walter's orbit during the period of the General Motors and Ford crises, never forgot his first meeting with Reuther. Mazey was conducting a meeting at which Walter was to speak. Mazey was about to perform the introduction when Walter drew him aside and explained just how he wanted this delicate matter handled. It was obvious to Mazey that here was a man who overlooked no detail, that here was a man who was going places fast.

The anecdotes about Walter's incredible energy are legion. On one occasion, in the late 1930's, some relatives persuaded Walter to take a day off to go with them to a cabin on Spider Lake in Northern Michigan. They had hardly arrived, as one of them later recalled, when "Walter spotted some little trees nearby. He thought they didn't look right there, so while everybody else headed for the lake, he marched into the brush with a hatchet."

Another time a neighbor happened to look out her window and see a strange man on the Reuther lawn, attacking weeds with a ferocity no weeds had ever encountered before. "May's got a wonderful new handy man," she told her husband excitedly. "Look at him go! I'm going to get his name." It was, of course, Walter.

This all-consuming passion to attack whatver engages his attention at the moment with the fury of the Rough Riders charging up San Juan Hill is one of Walter's most conspicuous traits. Aides at Solidarity House in Detroit still chuckle about the time they persuaded Walter to take a *real* vacation. He had, of course, never had one, and his assistants pointed out to him that, as a man who was forever advocating more leisure time for everybody, he should find out for himself what it was like. Protesting that *he* would be bored, Walter was finally persuaded and packed off to a Northern Michigan lake. A few days later he sent back a note: "I caught five fish on Monday, seven fish on Tuesday, and six fish today," it read, "and I'm going to catch all the fish in the lake before the end of the week." A friend chuckles at the memory. "Everyone's the big one for Walter," he says. "Everything's for keeps. He even goes after trout with all 20 guns roaring."

There is just no slowdown in Walter; he's always going full steam ahead. His wife says that if she finds him sitting she suspects he's sick—and, usually, she's right. Typically, Walter crams two days' work into one and thinks nothing of topping it all off with a five-to-seven-mile hike. Hike is the word for it, too; Walter never strolls. He swings along, bareheaded, his solid pouter-pigeon chest stuck out, his arms and legs pumping at a pace that would soon leave a Marine gasping. Back home after such a bracing finisher to his day, he steps under a cold shower to tone up all the capillaries, and finally tumbles into bed.

Even sleeping, however, Walter often refuses to stay quiet. His mind, like a clock, keeps running even in his dreams, and often it'll ring the bell with an idea. When this occurs, Walter is always ready. He keeps pad and pencil handy so that if an idea jolts him awake, he can jot it down before it escapes.

Such is the man. All of this furious energy, this ceaseless mental quest and drive, has given him an almost encyclopedic knowledge. Mention milk to him and he will cite figures, in gallons, on the comparative yield of Guernsey, Holstein, and Jersey cows. Admire the bird feeder in his backyard, and a lecture follows on the migratory habits of Michigan birds. "Ask Walter the time," said the late Spencer McCulloch of the St. Louis *Post-Dispatch,* "and he tells you how to make a watch."

Yet, with it all, his vision remains steady; his ideals and his goals are not greatly changed from those he adopted as a boy in those Sunday afternoon debates in his father's home in Wheeling. His major concern is people, their needs, their problems, what can be done to better the lot of the greatest number. He believes in what he describes as a "mixed economy"—an American version of the British Labour Party program, part socialization of key industries, part private enterprise; he believes in an "economy of abundance," which is almost certain to conflict quite sharply with the business community's undying faith in an economy of profit; and, above all, he has an absolute conviction of labor's right to a "bigger slice of a bigger pie" and an equally stout conviction that labor must use all its brains and ingenuity in helping to bring about this larger and better world of abundance for all.

Reuther's conviction that labor has a contribution to make in the realm of ideas and planning clashes with the most cherished belief of American business that only businessmen can understand the intricacies of business. Such matters as industrial capacity, production schedules, product costs, and sales prices—these, in the eyes of business, have always been the exclusive preserves of business and must remain so. What could labor leaders be expected to contribute to such intricate problems? The only excuse labor leaders have for existing—and an unfortunate excuse at that in the eyes of many businessmen—is to see that their workers get a few more cents an hour or a shorter work week. So goes most business thinking about the role of a labor leader.

It is the kind of thinking that reckons without Walter Reuther. Before him, most labor chieftains thought as management thought—that they should confine themselves to strictly labor problems. But not Reuther. He felt, and rightly, it would seem, that knowledge and ideas are not the exclusive preserve of any business or management class; he felt that his knowledge was as broad, his brain as swift as any executive's (swifter, perhaps, than most), and so he did not hesitate to defy management's most rigid taboo and inject his own ideas into the rarified atmosphere of executive row.

His first effort in this direction catapulted him into headline prominence from coast to coast. On December 23, 1940, he advanced the sensational suggestion that the idle and excess capacity of the Detroit assembly lines could be used to produce *500 planes a day*. The suggestion was made at one of the blackest hours of World War II, and it caught the imagination of the American people. Hitler's armies had overrun nearly all of Europe, and his air force was bombing Great Britain into a pulp. No one knew how long the overmatched British Royal Air Force could endure, how long the gritty British people could take the nightly pounding from the skies. Britain desperately needed war planes.

Reuther proposed a way to supply them. He pointed out that it would take months, years even, to build the new airplane plants the government had scheduled. This was time the free world could ill afford to waste. Yet the automotive assembly lines in Detroit were operating at only 50 percent of capacity, turning out 4,000,000 cars a year when they could produce 8,000,000. Reuther pointed out that there was not a great deal of difference between making a car motor and an airplane motor; the same basic types of machinery were used, the same kinds of labor, the same assembly-line techniques. Similarly, the body shops, assembly lines that could produce car chassis, could be converted to making plane wings and fuselages. Reuther urged that the various motor companies forget competition in the urgency of the hour, pool their resources, and unite with labor to turn excess plant capacity into the war production that was so badly needed.

At first Reuther's plan was widely hailed. President Roosevelt called it the kind of ingenuity the hour called for, and editorialists from coast to coast debated its soundness. It was a big breakthrough for Walter Reuther personally; for the first time, he appeared on the national scene not as the evil genius behind some obstructive sit-down strike, but as a labor statesman with brains and ideas and far ranging vision. Perhaps this was just the trouble. William Knudsen, who had been president of General Motors in the days of the Flint riots, had been called to Washington by Roosevelt as director of the Office of Production Management, and it soon became clear that Knudsen was not going to have any part of a Reuther Plan. He popped it quickly into his nearest pigeonhole, action that led Secretary of the Treasury Henry Morgenthau to remark acidly: "There is only one thing wrong with the [Reuther] program, it comes from the 'wrong source.'" And Charles E. Wilson, who had succeeded Knudsen as president of GM indicated business' peeve when he told Reuther: "If you are interested in production, I'll give you a job with us."

Clearly, the automotive industry wanted no part of three main ingredients of the Reuther Plan. It wanted no part of Reuther himself in his role of labor leader; it abhorred the idea that companies should pool resources with competitors; and it detested the suggestion that labor had ideas and should be consulted in cooperative planning. Reuther charged that the only reason his plan was not put into effect was that the companies wanted profits as usual and objected to having their plants drafted the way men were being drafted. In the end, after Pearl Harbor, a modified version of the Reuther Plan was put into effect, and Detroit became one of the mightiest elements in the "arsenal of democracy." But it did so very much on management's terms. Reuther and labor were kept well away from the conference board.

In the final analysis, most experts agree that Reuther's "500 planes a day," the figure that caught the popular imagination, was a decided exaggeration of Detroit's capabilities. But the basic features of his plan were sound, and the plan itself served at a highly critical moment to dramatize America's tremendous, almost incredible, industrial resources.

War, when it came, posed new problems for Walter Reuther and for all labor leadership. How should a union act? Should it suspend all wage demands? Should it give up its only weapon, the strike? Or should it adhere, as much of business seemed to be doing, to a "business-as-usual" attitude? These issues tore at the very fabric of the union during the war years. The UAW, in the end, adopted a two-pronged tactic. In large advertisements, it needled Knudsen and the Office of Production Management for their failure to consider the Reuther Plan and for allowing corporations to continue on a "business-as-usual" basis. At the same time, Reuther and other UAW leaders took a farsighted and highly patriotic view of labor's role. They decided on two major steps: strikes would be banned for the duration, and premium pay for work on Saturdays, Sundays, and holidays would be suspended.

This lofty stand provoked a bitter dispute in the ranks of labor. The leadership, which was united behind the proposals, split sharply with its own rank and file. This split became clear in an emergency conference called in April 1942. John McGill, speaking for the Flint Buick local, put the feelings of the workers bluntly when he said: "We are not convinced that giving up double time is necessary to winning the war. Labor is making sacrifices everywhere. We gave up the right to strike. Our brothers and sons are dying in the trenches. Can anyone show any sign that the men who sign checks have made any sacrifices?"

After bitter debate, and most unwillingly, the rank and file went along with its leadership, but throughout the union there was a sharp undercurrent of discontent. This was heightened as time went on, for the A. F. of L. had not thought it necessary to forego premium pay, and so it was only natural in some plant elections to choose union representation that the workers should vote to join an A. F. of L. union instead of the UAW.

The dissatisfaction mounted after the War Labor Board in July, 1942 put a tight ceiling on wages without imposing any similarly tight ceiling on profits. The wage rule limited increases to 15 per cent of the salary scales of January 1, 1941, regardless of how high the cost of living soared—and, under war pressures, it was rising steadily. War industries, on the other hand, were guaranteed a healthy margin of profit on every item they produced under the "cost-plus" formula. This meant simply that industry could tack its own healthy margin of profit on whatever an item cost, and the government would pay. It was a system that lent itself to rank abuses, for it quickly became obvious that, under it, the higher the costs might be, the higher the profit based on a percentage of cost certainly would be.

Now, in this situation, ironically enough, the selfish interests of management and the Communist Party merged in a most curious love affair. The Communists in the early days of the war, when Russia was not involved, had broken their backs trying to keep America neutral; but as soon as Russia was attacked by Hitler, they executed a flip-flop that would have stunned an acrobat. Overnight, they began to beat the drums for an ever mightier war effort, and early in 1943 they decided, great lovers of labor that they had always posed as being, that the time had come to sacrifice the interests of American labor to the interests of Stalin. In the cause of greater production to aid Russia, they advanced a program of "piecework" and "incentive pay."

The proposal, which would have benefitted both Communist political aims and management profits, all at the cost of the workers, can be understood only by an illustration. A standard time is set for performing a certain factory job. Suppose the standard calls for a worker to turn out two pieces of machinery in an eight-hour shift. For this he is paid $8. Suppose under a piecework system, by driving himself to his physical limit, he turns out four pieces of work. Normally you might think that he would be paid $16, but under the incentive pay plan, he was to get only $12; half of the extra $8 he had earned by faster work was to go to management. The War Production Board, under the direction of big business magnates, worked a further refinement. The Board proposed that incentive pay should be installed, not on an individual, but on a plant-wide basis. If an entire plant's output was increased, the percentage of pay savings would be distributed among the workers, even company presidents. The viciousness of such proposals is apparent. Not only would worker be set against worker in speedup competitions on the assembly lines, but the workers would get only a portion of the extra money to which they were rightfully entitled. Management would keep the rest and, under the WPB plan, presidents and executive office personnel, who almost certainly weren't going to be breaking their backs in any speedup, would have ridden the workers' shoulders to collect their percentage.

One would have to search hard to find a more vivid example of the truism that the far right and the far left, in their selfish preoccupations, so often become blood brothers. The Communist Party, abandoning its beloved workers, backed this vicious incentive-pay scheme for its own devious political ends; management loved it for its own greater profit. The cooperation between the two seems almost fantastic in retrospect, but it happened. Earl Browder, the Communist leader of the moment, declared: "It is patriotic to demand increased earnings based on increased production." He also made the incredible statement that "incentive pay" would "force better profits on unwilling employers."

Walter Reuther, who knew that there was no such animal as an unwilling employer where a greater profit was

[138]

concerned, angrily refused to have any part of the piecework-incentive pay scheme for which the Communists and management were soon beating such patriotic drums. He denounced it as a conscienceless exploitation of the worker, as a device that ultimately would wreck all labor unions, and soon the fur was flying in as furious a cat-and-dog fight as the UAW ever witnessed.

Browder let go with a scorching blast, attacking Reuther in a speech that was reprinted in a half-page advertisement in the *Detroit News*. He accused Reuther of attempted "wrecking" of the war effort and "of the most unprincipled demagogy and lying propaganda." Reuther, Browder charged, had "blocked the serious consideration" of incentive pay, had "forced the government to hesitate in bringing it forward," and had "created an ominous wave of strike sentiment. . . . " Production, he said, had been increasing steadily anyway, and he added: "If the workers had not been blocked by Reuther from establishing incentive pay rates, all of this increase in production would have meant increased wages for them. . . . "

The rank-and-file auto workers were not deceived. Reuther had damaged his own popularity with them by his no-strike and no-premium-pay stands in the first days of the war, but now he suddenly became the hero of workers who had suffered from brutal speedups on the assembly lines and who realized just what was at stake in the deceptive "incentive pay" propaganda. This sentiment was strengthened by moves in Washington, inspired by big business and backed by the Communist Party. War Manpower Commissioner Paul V. McNutt issued an order attempting to impose a wage freeze, and a bill, backed by big business and the military, which would actually have subjected labor to a rigid draft law, received the backing of Roosevelt and was introduced in Congress. These repressive measures added steam to the rank-and-file revolt, with the result that the whole "incentive pay" issue boiled up into one glorious free-for-all at the UAW convention held in Buffalo on October 4, 1943.

The Communist Party's drive to get the convention to back the piecework-incentive pay system was masterminded by two veteran unionists on the UAW executive board, George Addes and Richard Frankensteen. From the moment the convention session opened, it was evident that they were the targets of a large and vocal segment of the rank and file. Strong Reuther delegations came from Linden and Trenton, N.J., Buffalo, and New York City, and they made up a ditty that swept the convention like a popular song.

> Who are the boys who take their orders
> > Straight from the office of Joe Sta-leen?
> No one else but the gruesome twosome,
> > George F. Addes and Frankensteen.

> Who are the boys who fight for piecework,
> > To make the worker a machine?
> No one else but the gruesome twosome,
> > George F. Addes and Frankensteen.

> When it comes to double-talking,
> > Who is worse than Willie Green?
> No one else but the gruesome twosome,
> > George F. Addes and Frankensteen.

There were other verses, some unprintable, and they were roared all over Buffalo at all hours of the day and night. Regardless of the time, lines of delegates would form and snakedance through the corridors of hotels, blasting out with leather lungs "The Ballad of the Gruesome Twosome."

All of this was window dressing for the battle that broke out on the convention floor the instant the piecework issue was raised. "We fought nine years to eliminate piecework and haven't been able to do it yet," cried Richard Grosser, a UAW leader in Toledo. "You put it up now and, by God, our children's children won't eliminate it." The rafters rang with applause.

Another delegate, conceding that incentive pay might mean a small wage increase at the start, charged: "Our own bitter experience with it taught us that as we increase our earnings . . . management starts chopping down the standards to get our pay down again." Speech followed speech, and the bitterness of the workers became so evident that Addes, in presenting the piecework proposal, tried to cloak it in the robes of "democracy." He pointed out that some local unions had voted to try the piecework plan, and he argued that it would not be "democratic" to adopt a rule prohibiting outright their freedom to do so.

Here Walter Reuther sprang into the fray, ridiculing Addes' stand. "It is fine to talk about democracy," he said sarcastically. "Supposing a local union wanted to sign a wage agreement working 12 hours a day without overtime. Would you say that was interfering with local autonomy if it were stopped?"

The debate raged on for two days. R. J. Thomas, the union president, leaped astride the fence in a confusing speech that could be interpreted either way. In the end, the delegates adopted Reuther's resolution, opposing piecework and incentive pay in the UAW, and then they turned their attention to an effort to lift the scalps of Addes and Frankensteen. Addes managed to skin back into office as UAW secretary-treasurer by 70 votes out of 7,422 cast; but Reuther defeated Frankensteen by 346 votes in the race for first vice-president. Frankensteen had to settle for the second vice-presidency.

Reuther came out of the Buffalo convention a big winner, but his popularity was not yet the solid faith it later became. The no-strike pledge, reaffirmed at Buffalo with his support, continued to plague both him and the UAW. As the war continued, as prices and management profits mounted and wages remained frozen, the discontent among the mass of working unionists finally crystallized into an organization known as the "Rank and File Caucus." The Caucus wanted to junk the pledge, and in the UAW's last wartime convention in Grand Rapids, Mich., in September 1944, it fought a fierce floor battle that threw the UAW leadership into confusion. Unconditional retention of the no-strike pledge was championed by Nat Ganley, the Communist Party whip in the UAW, and Norman Mathews, a conservative leader. Reuther tried to adopt a middle course, favoring retention of the pledge only in those plants engaged in war production. The Caucus, of course, was for outright abolition.

In the showdown, Reuther's middle ground pleased nobody, and his proposal was roundly defeated. The Ganley-Mathews resolution failed to win a majority, and the Rank and File Caucus' ban polled 37 per cent of the vote. This left the UAW with no policy, much to the horror of its officers.

They finally called for a simple vote to keep the pledge until the entire union membership could ballot in a referendum. Reuther supported this plan and fought off the efforts of the Stalinists to avoid the referendum test. The convention finally voted with Reuther on the issue, but his stand cost him.

Though in the referendum two months later the rank and file of the union voted overwhelmingly to keep the no-strike policy, Reuther at Grand Rapids was loved by no one except his own dedicated followers. The Communists, of course, hated him; the Rank and File Caucus opposed him; and the conservative-minded shunned him. This combination of dislike and opposition cost him his first vice-presidency, as Frankensteen recaptured his former post by a vote of 5,444 to 4,528. Reuther had to settle for Frankensteen's vacated spot as second vice-president, and the convention as a whole probably marked the low point of his prestige and influence.

It was prestige and influence that he was not to regain until the war ended, striking off the shackles of restraint and leaving him free to operate again as an energetic and farseeing labor leader.

Chapter 10

The Labor Statesman

The end of World War II found labor spoiling for a chance to claim its proper share of the pie. Workers, of course, had made good money during the war. They had put in many hours of overtime which, even without premium pay, fattened the pay envelope. In many cases, both husbands and wives had found jobs on wartime assembly lines; and since civilian commodities were not being produced, many families came out of the war with savings larger than they had ever had. What then was labor's complaint?

It was simply this: wartime restrictions had held down its hourly pay scale, and with the coming of peace came the certainty that overtime would be cut back, that there would be an end to much of the husband-and-wife double job holding. When the switchover to civilian production began, labor found that jobs were downgraded to establish lower wage scales; bonuses were no longer given. Yet the cost of living remained astronomically high and showed signs of going higher. Though the rise in the labor wage scale had been frozen at 15 per cent of the January 1941, level, government statistics showed in June 1945, that food prices had risen 51 per cent. The overall cost-of-living, it was estimated, had jumped 45 per cent, and it was obvious that workers, with costs rising and pay frozen at a lower level, were soon going to be worse off than before.

Labor felt that it had been cheated. Two close and balanced observers of the UAW and Walter Reuther, Irving Howe and B. J. Widick, have written that "what was really at stake in the wartime discussions within the UAW was the question of what role unions should play in a war for which they were called upon to make sacrifices but from the control and direction of which they were rigorously excluded. By the war's end, the few posts that labor representatives had been given in Washington were either dissolved or rendered insignificant. It was clear that the war's economic program had been controlled by professional government experts and dollar-a-year industrialists." The result was a deep feeling that labor "could no longer function effectively if it limited itself to mere dollars-and-hours issues."

Walter Reuther saw this challenge more clearly than any other leader in the ranks of labor. As always, he had digested corporate reports and government statistics on the state of the economy. From these, he built a clear picture and raised his sights far above the immediate dollars-and-hours issues that concerned other labor leaders. Dollars and hours, Reuther saw, must be related to the health of the entire economy. His thinking was reflected in an economic brief he filed on June 30, 1945, with federal agencies in Washington. Hardly anybody paid much attention to it at the time. Most business and government officials dismissed it as just another Reuther "brainstorm." In this, they made a great mistake, for Reuther's central idea was both simple and sound.

"Labor contends," he wrote, "that the economic facts of life prove that wages can be increased without increasing prices. Increased production must be supported by increased consumption, and increased consumption will be possible only through increased wages. The basic question is: where will American labor's improved wage status come from?"

Reuther had a ready answer. Industry, he wrote, could "pay higher wages out of the high profits it is making. It will not have to charge higher prices."

Hardly had Japan surrendered on August 14, 1945, before Reuther translated this general philosophy into a program for action. On August 18, he submitted a preliminary brief to General Motors asking for *a 30 per cent wage increase without any increase in the price of cars!*

If Walter Reuther had maligned motherhood, he could not have produced a greater surge of outrage in the breast of GM. Business had been incensed at his meddling in its private preserves when he proposed his 500-planes-a-day formula, but that anger was a pale ghost beside the purple fury that swept the GM executive row when he presumed to suggest what price it should fix for its cars. It did not matter to GM that the welfare of the entire nation might be bound up in the issue, as it clearly was; all that mattered was that this bumptious, troublemaking redhead was sticking his nose into matters that were management's private concern.

Yet it should have been obvious even to GM that there was hard common sense behind Reuther's stand. Reuther

[147]

saw, as virtually all other labor and industrial leaders at the time refused to see, that labor would not benefit from a 30 per cent wage increase if the price on the products it produced was also going to leap 30 per cent. If each wage increase was to be followed by a price increase, the cost-of-living index would jump; more wage increases would be asked and, if granted, would lead to more price increases in an unending, vicious circle. This was the clear road to ruinous inflation. What Reuther sought was to tie the wage increase of the worker to improvements in production, to what GM could afford to pay and still make a generous profit. He said frankly that the union would accept less than a 30 per cent increase in pay if GM could prove it couldn't afford it, but if it was going to prove him wrong, it was going to have to open *all* its books.

This was the crowning affront. When negotiations between the company and the union opened in late October 1945, management negotiators were so infuriated that their prejudice and the narrowness of their viewpoint leaps from the lines of the transcript. Take this exchange between Harry Coen, GM assistant director of personnel, and Reuther:

COEN: There is nothing sincere in your approach. . . . It is just another chance for you to get up on a soapbox before more people . . .

REUTHER: Harry, if it was . . .

COEN: Keep quiet, will you? You are all wound up. Relax. I have been away hunting for a week. I am in good shape. I can look at this thing in its true perspective. . . . Is the UAW fighting the fight of the whole world?

[148]

REUTHER: We have been fighting to hold prices and increase purchasing power. We are making our little contribution in that respect.

COEN: Why don't you get down to your size and get down to the type of job you are supposed to be doing as a trade-union leader, and talk about money you would like to have for your people and let the labor statesmanship go to hell for awhile?

REUTHER: Translate it so I can know what you mean.

COEN: If you come to us and say, "We want X cents an hour," we can talk to you about whether we can give you X cents, or half of X or a quarter of X, or something like that. Instead of that you get off in your socialistic dreams, these Alice-in-Wonderland things of yours, and finally you get off to where you don't even understand yourself. . . .

The corporation's position at this point was coming through quite clearly, and Elwin Corbin, a UAW official, nailed it down hard in this exchange with Coen:

CORBIN: Do you mean if we came in here with a 30 per cent wage demand and offered to join with you in going before the Office of Price Administration for a 30 per cent increase in the price of your cars, you would talk business?

COEN: We don't ask you to join with us on the price of cars. It's none of your damned business what OPA does about prices.

CORBIN: The hell it isn't. I intend to buy a car.

This was the GM attitude. It was none of anybody's "damned business" what it did about the price of cars; yet

[149]

obviously it was, and had to be, everybody's business, everybody's concern. In a last effort to avoid a strike, Reuther offered to submit the union's case to arbitration, provided both sides would agree to open all books and consider the price problem. The corporation, charging that the union wanted "GM [to] relinquish its rights to manage its business," spurned the offer. The result: On November 21, 1945, some 200,000 workers in 96 GM plants laid down their tools. It was the first great strike of the postwar era, and it was to last for 113 days.

In contrast to the violent battles on the Flint picket lines less than ten years before, the strike was peaceful. General Motors did not try to use strikebreakers or to keep its production lines running; picketing became a formality. But the war of words, the bitter debate over principle, raged across the nation, with GM picturing itself as the champion of "free enterprise" against "union bosses" who sought to "tell us what we can make, when we can make it, where we can make it, and how much we can charge. . . . " This was, of course, a gross exaggeration of Reuther's position— just how much of an exaggeration he made clear in a stinging statement.

"The grim fact is," he said, "that if free enterprise in America is to survive, it has got to work; it must demonstrate more than an ability to create earnings for investment; it must master the technique for providing full employment at a high standard of living, rising year by year to keep pace with the annual increase in technological efficiency. . . . The fight of the General Motors workers is a fight to save truly free enterprise from death at the hands of its self-appointed champions."

The issues, it seems, were clearly drawn, but even so they were not properly understood in high places. President Harry S. Truman, for one, revealed little comprehension of the size of the stakes. He told the GM strikers to "return to work immediately" and declared that the strike was a "major obstacle holding up our reconversion program." The workers naturally resented his statement. The war was over; the time for one-sided sacrifice, they felt, had passed; and so they bluntly rejected the President's demand.

Rebuffed, Truman veered on a new course. He appointed a fact-finding board; but when he ruled that "ability to pay" should be one of the issues the board must consider, GM flatly refused to appear before it. On January 10, 1946, the board announced a decision that represented a clear-cut victory for the union. It held that GM could raise wages 19½ cents an hour without raising car prices. Though the board's figure was lower than the 30 per cent the union had asked, the UAW promptly announced it would accept the verdict. GM just as promptly rejected it.

The continuing deadlock now led to a general upheaval in the ranks of labor. By the end of January 1946, more than 1,650,000 industrial workers were marching on picket lines. Steel, packinghouse, electrical, and other industries were closed down. In the face of the growing debacle, the Truman administration, which had failed to exert its influence to obtain a quick settlement of the GM strike and establish a stable wage-price formula, now did a radical about-face. It let it be known that, if steel would settle, the administration would see that OPA would permit a rise in steel prices. Taking the hint, the CIO steel union settled for an 18½-cents-an-hour pay hike—with nothing said about prices.

This development helped to cut the ground out from under Reuther, but an even more treacherous blow soon was to be delivered. On February 12, 1946, the United Electrical Workers under the leadership of James Matles, known in labor as a follower of the Communist Party line, suddenly announced it had signed a contract with GM for the 30,000 workers under its jurisdiction. It had accepted the steel formula of 18½ cents an hour, even though this was below the figure the Presidential fact-finding board had recommended for GM. The UAW, which had not even been informed its fellow union was talking secretly with GM, charged an outright double cross, and the sneak settlement by the electrical workers was widely seen as a devious Communist Party maneuver to ruin Reuther's prestige by saddling him with a lost strike.

The effect, certainly, was damaging, and as time went on it became increasingly apparent that Reuther was fighting a lone battle. No other labor leaders had the vision to see what he saw—that pay increases would mean little or nothing to labor if they were all to be eaten up by higher prices. Most labor leaders fitted into the role management allotted them, bargainers for higher wages, and they did not concern themselves about what happened to the rest of the economy. Even Philip Murray, who had become president of the CIO, disliked Reuther's wage and anti-inflation formula, and urged him to drop it. The heads of the Ford and Chrysler divisions of the UAW backed Murray. This cooling of top-level union leadership to Reuther's strategy angered many of the strikers walking the picket lines. "I wouldn't mind losing to GM," said one, "nearly so much as I mind being slapped in the face by the president of the CIO."

In the end, Reuther and the UAW had to settle for the 18½-cent formula that had been negotiated behind their backs. They had won a wage increase for labor, but they had lost the larger battle. For the Truman administration, after the steel settlement, had permitted a $5-a-ton increase in the price of steel; the steel hike increased the cost of autos that were made of steel; and the postwar inflation spiral was off and running.

Not until the consequences had become obvious did the masterminds of the corporate and governmental worlds begin to worry about the inflationary problem that had so concerned Reuther. But by that time the opportunity to prevent the damage and create a balanced economy had been lost. Walter Reuther had been too far ahead of the thinking of his day to win the immediate battle, but he had emerged from the first great postwar strike as the boldest and most imaginative labor leader in America. It was obvious to most thinking observers that greater things lay in his future.

Chapter *11*

Final Leap to Power

T he UAW opened its 1946 convention in the Convention Hall at Atlantic City, N.J., on March 23, just ten days after the settlement of the General Motors strike. It was one of those freewheeling, uproarious affairs for which the UAW had become noted; but this time it was even more so than usual. For everyone knew that this was the showdown. This was the year Walter Reuther was going to make his big bid to oust R. J. Thomas from the presidency.

Reuther's campaign had begun in Detroit even while the GM strike was on, and the tactics of the Communists in undercutting his position by their secret settlement with GM had added steam to it. Reuther and the Communists had been at dagger's point for years. As the Communist Party was later to proclaim in a frank resolution: "Since 1939 our main line has been to weld a progressive coalition of communist and non-communist auto workers to isolate and defeat the Reuther policy and leadership. . . . " In pursuit of this goal, the Communists had developed their influence to the point where they dominated the UAW executive board. High officers of the union owed their positions to Communist support—and they knew it. Reuther was determined to put an end to this, to purge the Communists and their stooges and drive them from their positions of influence.

As the delegates poured into Atlantic City, the Reuther forces held caucus after caucus. These meetings were not just to count noses and map immediate strategy; they were also sessions of political indoctrination. Reuther, tireless, bursting with ideas, lucid and persuasive as a speaker, was at his magnetic best. He spoke to delegation after delegation, hammering home the point that the Communists were stooges of Moscow and that they would sell out labor any time it suited their political line. He had impressive illustrations to prove his thesis—the Communist campaign for "piecework" and "incentive pay" in wartime, the Communist backing of the proposed labor draft law, the Communist sellout in the recent GM strike.

This was the kind of talk that fueled and fired the troops, and soon the Atlantic City boardwalk became a scene of bedlam. Rival factions, fists cocked, met and clashed in scrimmages along the boardwalk and in the bars, where informal troupes of Walter's boys could almost always be found doing a buck-and-wing and chanting, "Reuther, Reuther, rah, rah, rah!" On the floor of the convention, every time a Communist delegate rose to speak, the Reutherites went "Quack! Quack! Quack!"

Between the chanting and the quacking, the Communists marshalled all their legions in a grim, last-ditch attempt to save R. J. Thomas. Thomas was not himself a Communist; he had risen to the union presidency as a compromise candidate between the Communist and non-Communist elements. But the Communists had been extremely happy with him, and it was not hard to see why. Thomas was the kind of brawny, shortsighted labor leader who towered like a hero in a picket-line brawl but lost his effectiveness when he had to choose among complex issues. It was widely recognized in the UAW that when Reuther talked about the wage-price relationship in the battle to keep inflation down and boost purchasing power, Thomas had only the foggiest idea why he was so excited. Getting more money for his men and cutting down the work week were the kind of simple objectives Thomas could understand. The intricacies of economics were just too much for him, and he seemed to have no conception that he was being led around by the nose—that his closest associates in the UAW hierarchy, Addes, Frankensteen, and Richard Leonard, all had been playing the game of the Communist forces and owed their positions in great part to Communist backing.

Knowing Thomas for a blundering innocent in the ideological wilderness, the Reuther forces got out a pamphlet in which they challenged the embattled UAW president to a public debate with their leader. Addes was in the chair when the proposal was made on the convention floor, and he quickly discovered a rule in the bylaws that said such a debate would have to be approved by a two-thirds vote of the delegates. Addes then called for a standing vote, which he as chairman alone would interpret; and though it seemed to many observers that more than two-thirds voted for the debate, Addes ruled to the contrary, refused a roll call—and so temporarily saved Thomas.

This shunning of a direct face-to-face test was hardly calculated to win favor for Thomas in such a freewheeling union; and the Thomas forces, increasingly desperate, began to pin their faith on Philip Murray. The CIO chieftain was to deliver a major address to the convention, and it was well known that he did not particularly like Walter Reuther— that, indeed, he hadn't understood the logic behind Reuther's wage-price policy much better than R. J. Thomas had. Murray, however, had a great reputation among union men everywhere; his words would carry weight with many delegates; and so speculation grew as to whether he would endorse Thomas.

All through his speech, while the delegates hung on every word, Murray gave no indication where his sympathies lay. He came to the close, and in the very last lines, he distributed impartial thanks to all the officers of the union in a curiously partial way. He wanted, he said, to express his gratitude to all—"to Secretary Addes, Vice-President Reuther, Vice-President Frankensteen, and to this great big guy for whom I have a distinct fondness, the President of your Union, R. J. Thomas. . . ."

The Thomas cohorts lapped it up. Murray's acknowledgement that his heart was moved for their "great big guy" should swing enough votes, they thought, to bury the candidacy of the presumptuous Walter Reuther. In most circumstances, it probably would have; but the memory of the Communist sellout in the GM strike was fresh and raw, and Reuther had done his work well in making it crystal clear just what had happened, what forces had been responsible. He felt confident. Just before the vote, he went up to Thomas and offered to shake hands. Thomas, in a huff,

[158]

Reuther supporters elevating the new president of the UAW

refused the goodwill gesture, and Walter, not at all put out by the rebuff, checked the "great big guy" off with one of those lightning-fast Reuther sallies. "Tommy," he said, "if you're not big enough to lose, you're not big enough to win."

And so it proved. When the votes were counted, Walter won the presidency by 4,444 to 4,320. His deliriously happy followers hoisted him on their shoulders in a victory parade, and Walter himself was so moved and so happy he actually broke all his training rules and did an unprecedented thing. He sipped a beer and took a couple of puffs on a big cigar. The rejoicing, though justified, proved a bit premature. For the UAW next made a bewildering move. After electing Reuther, the delegates turned right around and voted back into office the very pro-Communist officers and executive board members Walter had been fighting. As a result Walter found himself heading a crew, two-thirds of whom were sworn to dump him overboard at the first chance.

What followed was one of the zaniest years in all UAW history. Walter managed, by clever dealing, to squeeze two key appointments through the executive board. He got his professorial brother, Victor, appointed the union's educational director, and he managed to install big, genial Frank Winn, who was much respected by all newspapermen, as the union's public relations director. But there Walter's influence stopped. The executive board, in the complete grip of his enemies, decided he was entitled to his paycheck and nothing else. They refused even to tell him what they were doing.

Communist propaganda was released to the press as official union policy statements, and the first Walter would know of it was when he read the news in the papers. The executive board even went so far as to petition Congress to rename the Taft-Hartley Act, much hated by labor, "the Taft-Hartley-Reuther Act" on the grounds that Reuther was more anti-labor then either of the act's actual authors.

The nonsense became wilder and wilder. Walter's Communist opposition planted the rumor that he was going to run for vice president in 1948 on a Republican ticket headed by Senator Robert A. Taft, of Ohio; they spread the canard that he was anti-Semitic and a follower of the rabble-rousing Gerald L. K. Smith. At board meetings, he was literally, physically pushed around, and even Phil Murray, seeing the light, confessed that the internal struggle in the UAW had "sunk to the level of complete moral degeneracy."

Walter, whose personality is almost irresistible if a man is subjected to it long enough, turned the full battery of his charm on Murray, and they were soon "Phil" and "Walter" to each other. Having thus solidified relations at the top, Walter tore all around Detroit, talking as he says "to thousands of guys all over this town," to make clear to the ranks the danger and the evil of Communist influence in the union. In addition, he found time to finecomb the union's bylaws, and so he made a momentous discovery. Checks, the bylaws said, weren't good unless signed by the president.

This meant that Addes, the anti-Reuther secretary-treasurer of the union, was not the sole financial power. Waving the bylaws, Reuther charged before the hostile executive board and demanded control of the books. The board told him what he could do with his bylaws. Refusing the advice, Walter got on the telephone and notified the banks that no draft on the UAW treasury was good until he had given the cashier the check number over the phone.

[161]

This was a roadblock the executive board hadn't counted on, and while they huddled with their lawyers, Walter scanned checks and phoned the numbers of the ones he approved to the banks.

Control of the purse strings usually means control, period. The board discovered from its lawyers that there was no way to loosen Walter's hold on the union's finances while he was around, but the happy thought occurred to them that, when he was absent, as he frequently was, there would be plenty of opportunity to raid the till. So they had a rubber stamp made up with a facsimile of Walter's signature on it. Walter was ready for that one. He called in the conspiring opposition and laid down the law. Unless he got some cooperation, he said, he was just going to stop signing the pay checks for the members of the executive board. "Those fellows hated my guts," Walter chuckles, "but they loved their pay checks. They came through."

Walter was now building for the final showdown at the 1947 convention; so were his Communist-led opponents. They devised a dandy gimmick. A little farm-equipment workers' union wanted to join the UAW. The executive board decided its application was made to order; the board would get the UAW to admit the union, then it would give the new outfit the entirely unwarranted number of 500 delegates (all delightfully anti-Reuther, of course), and with this extra 500 votes, it would bury Walter. In this, it reckoned, of course, without Walter, who has a strong aversion to being buried.

He raced all over Detroit, speaking at union meetings, exposing the fakery that was being engineered. He was so tireless and so persuasive that auto workers everywhere got the point, and when a referendum was held on admitting the new union, the workers turned down the idea by a vote of better than two to one. That practically doomed Walter's opposition. Not only had its ruse failed, but it had been exposed and bowled over by the boomerang.

The UAW convention that convened on November 9, 1947, was, as a result, almost humdrum. The workers had had enough of the Communist element's shenanigans, and they were now solidly, overwhelmingly, in Walter's camp. He swept back into office, and this time his victory was complete. His slate captured 18 of the 22 seats on the executive board.

Walter set out at once to clean house. Back in Detroit, he fired Communist sympathizers in brigade lots, cleared out drones, opened a campaign to drive lottery operators out of the factories, and prepared for a militant stand in new negotiating sessions that were soon to open. These were actions that stepped on innumerable toes, and there can be no doubt that many who were hurt hated Walter.

He and May were then living at 20101 Appoline Street. After five years in little apartments with May's parents, Walter, who had never drawn a big union salary, had managed to save $1,265. It was enough for a down payment on a $7,750 white brick-and-frame bungalow with maple furniture, ruffled curtains, and a basement workshop. There was an upstairs bedroom for the Reuthers' five-year-old daughter and another spare bedroom downstairs for her infant sister. The kitchen was in the rear of the house, and when Walter came home in the evening, usually late, he would prowl around carefully so as not to wake the children while May made supper and he told about his day.

[163]

At 9:30 on the cool evening of April 20, 1948, Walter had just finished a dish of stew and was standing by the refrigerator, holding a bowl of preserved fruit. May asked him a casual question. He turned to answer her. As he did, there was an ear-shattering roar in the back yard. It came from a 12-gauge shotgun, loaded with buckshot, both barrels fired almost simultaneously.

The blast crashed through the storm sash and glass of the kitchen window. Caught in the hail of pellets, Walter pitched forward on the floor, his right arm nearly severed, crying in a mixture of surprise and agony; "They shot me, May!"

Chapter 12

In the Shadow of Murder

Walter Reuther had been all but killed. He lay on his back partly under the kitchen table, his right arm flopping helplessly, unable to move. May rushed to the telephone. Neighbors, who had heard the shotgun's roar, hurried in. One of them dashed away and returned with a neighborhood doctor who staunched the bleeding of Walter's wounds, put his arm in an emergency splint, and gave him a shot of morphine to deaden the pain. Through it all, Walter was conscious—and angry. "They had to shoot me in the back," he muttered. "They couldn't come out in the open and fight."

An ambulance came, and Walter was rushed to New Grace Hospital. There Prosecutor James N. McNally questioned him to find out if he had any idea who the "they" might be. Walter told him: "In the early days I used to get all sorts of threats. I haven't got a threatening letter or anything like that in a number of years. During the past week I debated with Senator Taft on a national hookup and since then I got a flood of mail, about 98 per cent favorable, and the other 2 per cent disagreed, but nothing that could be associated with this. In the early days we had a fight with industry and maybe there is some industry move behind this, but I am not prepared to say that. I say that it is possible.

"Another possibility is the Communists might have done it. I don't know that for sure. It is true I have fought them very hard and I think successfully in the last year, and that didn't make them happy at all.

"It may have been also some people I term outright reactionaries or Fascists who would disagree with me as much as the Communists, because six or eight years ago I used to get crank letters, but I have had nothing like that in the last several years. This thing tonight came without any realization of it at all."

The subsequent police investigation showed clearly just how lucky Walter was to be alive. In the grass-covered backyard, police discovered three heel prints pressed so deeply into the sod that it was obvious the gunman had been standing for a long time in one place, waiting. Ordinarily, Walter parked his car on a side street, opened a gate in the white picket fence, and came up a concrete walk to the kitchen door. Had he followed this normal route on the evening of the shooting, he would have walked almost into the muzzle of the waiting shotgun—and certain death. But on this night, for no particular reason that he could remember, he had just happened to stop his car in front of the house, entering through the front door. This slight change in his routine had compelled the lurking gunman to wait and to attempt to make the much more difficult shot through the closed kitchen window.

Even then, only the luckiest of chances had saved Walter, for the gunman's aim had been professionally deadly. The murderous blast of his shotgun would have caught Walter across the full width of his back, riddling him, except that in the last split second Walter turned to look at May and answer her question. This turn saved his life. Four pellets shattered his right arm, a fifth plowed through his chest from right to left; but the bulk of the shot passed him by, perforating the kitchen cupboard, a ventilator, and the plaster on the wall.

These details convinced police that a professional underworld thug had been responsible for the deed, but this was as far as they got. They took casts of the heel prints in the sod. Rewards totaling $117,800—the largest in a criminal case in America up to that time—were offered for information leading to the arrest of the gunman. Hundreds of tips poured in; hundreds of witnesses were questioned. The result was a dead end, nothing.

Walter's condition was grave for several days, but it soon became clear he wasn't going to die, though it was questionable whether we would ever be able to use his right arm again. His mother, Anna, rushed up from Wheeling, and she and May kept a constant vigil at his bedside. The sight of her son, torn by buckshot, struggling for life, did something to Anna Reuther. She was a courageous, indomitable woman, and she had lived her life possessed by the strong union faith of all the Reuthers. But this was too much. She remembers sitting by Walter's bedside in the hospital one day and begging him to quit. "Go into some other

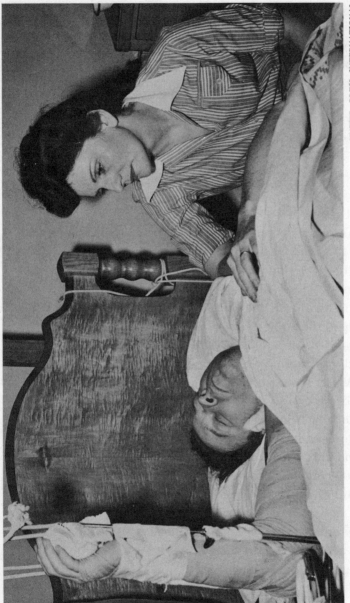

May visiting Walter in the hospital after the shooting

work," she told him. "Give this up. You could write books, or go back to your trade. You would make just as much money."

Walter looked startled. "I'd make *more* money," he said weakly.

"Then do it," Anna urged.

There was a pause. Then Walter shook his head. "No," he murmured, "I'm all tied up in this thing, all involved. I must do it."

His voice faltered, and Anna caught a disconnected phrase, one that all the Reuther boys had inherited from their father, "the brotherhood of man." Then Walter drifted off into unconsciousness.

May, sitting across the bed from Anna, looked at her and said, "Don't you see he must do it? You must understand."

Anna understood. She knew her Reuther brood. Afterwards, she told Walter, "I feel worried about you, but I want you to know that, whatever happens to you, I want you to do what you think is right. Even if you lose your life."

This was more like Reuther talk, and Walter remembers it with gratitude. "Mother," he says, "was a tower of strength." Walter needed such support. He was in constant and excruciating pain. Surgeons had pieced the shattered bones in his arm together as best they could, but nobody knew whether the arm itself could be saved, or, if it was, if it would ever again be useful. The upper part of Walter's body was in a cast, and the arm itself was raised, in traction. Little morphine could be given him to deaden the pain because the doctors were fearful it would slow his circulation. Periodically, electric shock treatments were given the injured arm to keep the damaged muscles and nerves from decaying. At these times the agony became almost unbearable. And all the time there were other worries.

The shooting was a national sensation. Appoline Street became a sightseer's paradise. Crowds formed, milled about the Reuther home, gaping at the free show. Popcorn vendors set up shop on the sidewalk. Walter, at first, knew nothing about all this; he learned about it the hard way, from his older daughter, Linda. "Daddy," she asked him one day while visiting him in the hospital, "why can't they leave us alone? Why can't I be like other kids?"

Besides family problems, Walter, as always, had the union on his mind. The shooting had come at a critical time. The climate throughout the nation was bad for unions. Some strikes had been broken; some unions were tied up in court battles; others seemed timid and uncertain. And all the time prices, as a result of that break in the dam the Truman administration had allowed in 1946, were soaring at a pace that made the wartime rise look like a slow crawl. Another wage increase was necessary for labor, and Walter, at the moment he was gunned down, had been preparing to move against Chrysler, General Motors, and Ford.

With Walter incapacitated, Emil Mazey took over as acting president. Not as colorful as Walter, but vigorous and forceful, Mazey led the union in a strike against Chrysler on May 12, 1948. At the same time he threatened to strike General Motors; and GM, seeing that the UAW had made its Chrysler picket lines effective, yielded. Its package included an immediate six cents an hour wage increase and, more important, an escalator clause providing workers with automatic increases should the cost of living continue to rise.

This provision, highly controversial at the time, later was to become a fixture in many union contracts.

Walter was now out of the hospital, but his body was still in a cast, his shattered arm supported by a steel brace. As soon as he could, he moved his family from the white brick bungalow on Appoline Street that had been his and May's first real home. The union supplied him with body-guards and insisted, much to his disgust, in providing him with a heavily armored, bulletproof $12,000 Packard sedan. All of these precautions, as it turned out, were no safeguard against what was to happen next.

On the night of May 22, 1949, Victor Reuther was sitting in the living room of his home with his wife, Sophie. There had been some disturbance in the neighborhood lately. Victor and his wife had had a small cocker spaniel that had taken to barking urgently in the yard at night. The dog was small, his bark wasn't much of a bark, and so the Reuthers had been surprised when a policeman called, informed them there had been an anonymous complaint and they'd have to get rid of the dog. The next day, the policeman had returned; there had been another anonymous complaint. And so reluctantly, yielding to the law, the Reuthers had given away the dog.

All was quiet, as a result, on this particular night. Sophie had been mending, Victor reading the New York *Times Magazine*. Suddenly, the bulb in the lamp by Sophie's chair went out, and Victor rose, got another bulb and screwed it into the lamp. As the bright light came on— "illuminating the target," as Victor later observed dryly— a shotgun roared from the yard. The blast caught Victor full in the face. For a moment, he remembers, he thought the

[171]

light bulb had exploded; then he pitched downward into darkness. Sophie ran out of the house, screaming, "My God, Vic's been shot!"

Neighbors rushed out of their houses just in time to see a man sprint across the lawn, jump into a maroon car, and speed away. Behind him in the shrubbery he had left a 12-gauge shotgun, the same type of weapon, perhaps the same gun, that had mowed down Walter a year earlier.

Informed of the shooting, Walter rushed to the hospital, his own maimed arm still in a sling. "It's not possible," he said in first, shocked disbelief. "Not both of us. Not twice." It was, unfortunately, not only possible, but a fact. Victor Reuther was in desperate plight. Two pea-sized slugs had lodged in his throat, one in his mouth; a fourth had destroyed his right eye. "For several days, it was touch and go whether Vic was going to live or not," Walter says. But Victor lived. The Reuthers, Anna Reuther explains, have "good blood." Perhaps. Indisputably, they also have something else—courage. Despite the loss of one eye, despite the slugs in his throat, Victor still had the colossal guts to joke. "It's a good thing they didn't shoot out my tongue," he said. "I couldn't make a living."

In the wake of this second shooting, the reward offers were boosted to $250,000. Even this did no good. The UAW, taking a dim view of some of the police work, eventually hired its own detectives, and they, perhaps, came closest to solving the mystery.

Five years later, one of the UAW detectives located an apparently knowledgeable Canadian hoodlum. After much persuasion, the Canadian signed a confession in which he said he had ridden with two other men to Walter's house the

[172]

night Walter was shot. The informant named the other men, said he had been paid $5,000 for his part in the job, and told who paid him.

It seemed that the UAW sleuth had located the key witness. Authorities at once took the informant into protective custody and issued warrants for the arrest of the men he had named. Then a strange thing happened. The indispensable witness, who was being held under police guard in a hotel, told his custodians he was going to take a shower. Wearing his coat and hat, novel attire for showering, he went into the bathroom. In a moment, the water came on hard; it ran that way for almost an hour before it finally dawned on the guards that their man was taking an exceptionally long shower. They then went and looked. They found an empty bathroom. Their man, after turning on the shower, had kept right on going—out another door and across the border into Canada.

In the post mortems, it developed that the UAW had deposited a down payment of $5,000 for the man who knew all. His girl friend had managed to collect the money, and when the informer joined her, he and she had a gay fling. When police finally caught up with the pair, the gentleman promptly repudiated his confession, denied all, and fought extradition back to the United States. And that was that.

Was it all a hoax? Or was the confession, despite its author's later denying it, the true story? A number of supporting details make the UAW think to this day that their detective was probably on the right track. According to the Canadian, he and his hoodlum companions were hired by a Detroit underworld character, a onetime rumrunner who specialized in strong-arm assignments and had acquired an unsavory reputation as a union-buster. Now it just so happened that one of Detroit's auto-parts manufacturers had concluded a service contract with this same union-wrecker's son-in-law. It was a very strange deal. The contract came to nearly $100,000 more than the auto-parts firm had been paying the previous holder, and Mr. Tough's son-in-law performed no services—he just pocketed the extra boodle and leased the job itself right back to the original holder of the contract. Why all the shenanigans?

Well, the auto-parts corporation, a big one, was having contract trouble with its UAW local. The union wanted more money. The corporation didn't want to pay it. Things got very rough. All of a sudden (no one could say, of course, that there was any connection with the contract that had fed some $100,000 into underworld hands) there was an outbreak of violence; a number of persons were beaten up. "All of the people who were beaten up were union people," Frank Winn says. "Two of them were damn near killed, and the only reason for it that we could find was that they represented a militant force in the union. Both of them, incidentally, were strong supporters of Walter's."

Walter himself had nothing to do with the contract negotiations, but he was the boss and the brains of the UAW, the much hated symbol of management's trouble. Killing him, it may have been reasoned, would so disorganize the union, so cow the workers and shatter their morale, that contracts could be dictated on management's terms. This, to the UAW, still seems like the likeliest explanation, and it is reinforced by one other bit of striking evidence. During the Christmas season of 1949, a reporter for the Detroit *Times* got an anonymous telephone tip that UAW headquarters was

[174]

to be blown up. A search uncovered 39 sticks of dynamite, taped into three bundles. Quite obviously someone was playing rough—and for keeps.

Who that someone was can not now ever be legally established. The legal time limit for the prosecution of the man, or men, who shot the Reuthers has passed, and no action can ever be brought against them.

Since this is so, since the shotgun marksman who just missed killing both Reuthers may still be alive and at large, Walter has had to live his life ever since that year of horror—the year of "accidents," as the Reuthers call it—under constant guard every minute of the day and night. Watchdogs and guards protect his home; guards travel with him wherever he goes.

Chapter **13**

Still Going Strong

Walter Reuther built himself back to health by building a house. It took long, agonizing months for the bones in his shattered right arm to knit and for the muscles to regain their strength. Even after he had shed his steel brace and sling, his arm and hand had that withered look that results from muscles and flesh wasting in confinement. A doctor told him that if he was not to have a claw hand, he must exercise constantly to stretch the fingers; and so, like many another in such circumstances, he kept squeezing a rubber ball. And to restore the strength of his arm, he hammered nails until the tears came.

Since the nail hammering seemed an essential exercise for his aching arm, Walter decided that he might as well hammer to some purpose. After the retreat from Appoline Street, he and his family lived for a time in an increasingly Negro neighborhood. Summers, however, were a problem, for landlords of cottages in the country were fearful the Reuthers might bring gunfire with them. So Walter bought a tract of land on a winding trout stream. On the property was a run-down, one-room cabin. Walter decided to build up his muscles by making the cabin livable.

At the end of four years, no one would ever have known that a shotgun blast had nearly separated his right arm from his body, and the cabin had been made so comfortable that the Reuthers decided to live in the country the year-round. This meant more furious activity for Walter. He began to do more work, to add on rooms, build a second story, construct bridges.

The location of Walter's home remains a loosely held secret. For his own protection, the site is never identified except to say that it is in the countryside some 35 miles northwest of Detroit. From the road all that can be seen is a white house that looks like a farmhouse (it isn't, it's a barracks for Walter's guards). A tall steel fence, with a padlocked gate, surrounds the property. Inside the gate is the sound of quick water—"my moat," Walter calls it. Actually, it is a 30-foot wide trout stream that makes three tight, hairpin turns in a small area. The Reuther home lies in the elbow of the third bend, and to reach it one crosses three bridges. Walter built the bridges. He also designed and built the long redwood house. He built the furniture. An elaborate hi-fi set is his creation. So are the built-in book cases within arm's reach of the deep easy chairs; accordion doors of hinged walnut that open on washrooms; low cabinets finished with boiled linseed oil because, Walter explains, this makes them easy to repair if they're scratched.

It is a home that any man might be proud of and one that few men could have built with their own hands, rebuilding themselves in the process. But it is also a home that has about it something of the atmosphere of a voluntary prison. The picture windows are made of bulletproof glass. Four big watchdogs, two in and two out, prowl the perimeter of the steel fence. Guards are on duty round the clock. All of these are precautions that are still necessary despite the fact that, in the years since the shooting, Walter has become one of the two dominant labor leaders in America.

In early November, 1952 Phillip Murray was stricken with a heart attack in San Francisco and was found dead on the floor of his hotel room. Allan S. Haywood, long his close associate and executive vice president of the CIO, seemed in line to succeed him, but the man with a stronger following among the labor legions was Walter Reuther. He had the solid backing of the big automobile unions; he also had the support of the influential Newspaper Guild of America. In another uproarious Atlantic City convention, he defeated Haywood and became president of the second largest labor organization in America.

Walter made it clear in his acceptance speech—if it had not been clear before—that he intended to be a different type of labor leader. Though many union presidents like John L. Lewis were drawing down salaries of $75,000 a year, Reuther announced he would be content with the extremely modest $11,250 the UAW was paying him. He has since advanced into the $20,000-a-year bracket, but his salary would still be despised by any self-respecting officer heading a corporation.

This renunciation of money for the privilege of working a 12-to-18 hour day is typical of Walter Reuther and a sign of his dedication. Other signs were sprinkled through

Reuther before a portrait of the late Philip Murray

that acceptance address. Walter announced that he hoped to bring about a merger of the CIO with the numerically more powerful AFL headed by George L. Meany, a merger that has since become a reality, with Meany as President and Reuther Vice-President of the combined organization. Then he went on, in terms that were purest Reuther, to give his vision of the world and of labor's place in it.

"There is a revolution going on in the world," he said. "The Communists didn't start that revolution. It is a revolution of hungry men to get the wrinkles out of their empty bellies. It is a revolution of people who have been exploited by imperialism to throw off the shackles of imperialism and colonialism, and to march forward in freedom and independence. It is a struggle of the have-nots to get something for themselves. The Communists didn't start it. They are riding its back. . . .

"You see, man is an economic being. He has to have food and clothing, housing and medical care and all the other material needs, and we struggle to make that possible. But man is more than an economic being. He is a spiritual being, and just as food is needed for the economic man so the spiritual man needs food, and freedom is food of the soul. The great challenge in the world is to find a way so that man can so arrange relationship of one to the other within one society, and one nation to another in a world society, so that we can live in peace and harness the power of technology and exploit our resources and translate that into the good life for everyone. . . ."

The "good life for everyone" remains Walter's goal. It's a theme that runs through almost every sentence he utters whether on the platform or in private conversation. His

[181]

mind, it seems, is always teeming with projects to bring that "good life" closer to realization. One of these pet projects, which he began to trumpet in the fall of 1954, was the idea of a "'guaranteed annual wage" in the automobile industry.

Traditionally, the industry had been for labor a feast-or-famine existence. During model changeover periods, the production lines were shut down and workers were laid off by the thousands; when retooling had been completed and new models were ready to roll, the production lines hummed again and workers were rehired by the thousands. Walter believed that proper planning by management could avoid this disruption, that the shift to new models could be made more gradually, and that, in any event, the motor companies should pay their workers a basic compensation during such layoff periods, thus guaranteeing a basic annual income.

With major auto contracts expiring in the spring of 1955, Walter concentrated on Ford. There the management, after the capitulation and later the death of Henry Ford, had switched from being the most reactionary to being the most idealistic in the industry. Ford, Walter felt, could be brought to agreement first; then General Motors and Chrysler would have to follow.

Showdown negotiating sessions are meat and drink to Walter. William Manchester has written this description:

"At bargaining sessions Walter is very much in his Detroit role. The meetings are staged around long, brilliantly lit tables; outside there are switchboards, recording devices and private lines to relay new proposals from the other side.

"The union negotiates with Ford, General Motors and Chrysler simultaneously, in different parts of town, but the tip-off that Walter has picked his prey comes when he stows his briefcase and toothbrush under one table.

"After that things get rough. The final stretch may last forty hours without a break—he once suggested cheerily that General Motors hew out a tunnel from their office building to him—and a man with his constitution has a big edge."

The negotiations with Ford for the guaranteed annual wage in 1955 followed this typical Reuther pattern. For some two weeks before the final showdown, Walter kept recharging his batteries on only two or three hours sleep a night, yet he never seemed to run down. He exuded energy, vitality, confidence. Watching him roaring full speed ahead, a veteran Detroit newspaperman perhaps put his finger on the source of Walter's unflagging energy and joyous zest in combat. "The Big Boy," he said, "enjoys nothing so much as making a monkey out of the fat cats."

Ford, it seemed, was rigid. The guaranteed annual wage was a heresy not even to be considered. Walter brushed off these protests the way one deals with a swarm of gnats, stowed his briefcase and toothbrush under the Ford table, and went into that final knock-'em-down, drag-'em-out battle with Ford Vice President John Bugas. He put his cards right on the table and let Bugas stare at them. A crippling strike, he pointed out, had started the decline of the Willys-Overland Company. Chrysler had been drawing up on Ford as the No. 2 auto producer when it had been shut down by a 102-day strike in 1950. Ford didn't want such things to happen to Ford, did it?

The session lasted 26 hours. When it was over, Reuther had the basis of his guaranteed annual wage, for Ford had agreed to grant its workers semiannual layoff pay. A swarm

[183]

En route to the Ford negotiations, 1955

Announcing the new Ford contract, 1955

of weary, haggard Detroit newspapermen were waiting to get the details as the marathon conference broke up. Bugas emerged from the conference room first, looking drawn and haggard as if he'd just been pulled through the keyhole. Then came Walter Reuther, bright and chipper, looking like a man who has just had a good night's sleep and has just stepped out of a refreshing shower. While Bugas retired to a corner and leaned against a wall for support, Walter barged full steam ahead into a session with the waiting newsmen. His mind was already racing toward the future.

"We'll shoot for a shorter week," he said, "but how much shorter is impossible to say now. These things can't be arbitrary. . . . A shorter work week must flow from the fact that science and technology will have given us the tools to create greater wealth with less effort and time.

"Personally, I'd favor a four-day, thirty-two-hour week over six hours a day, five days a week. Then you begin to give people the real benefits of progress through a long weekend."

Wouldn't labor ever be satisfied? someone asked. Walter had heard this many times before, and he had the pat answer. "You know," he said, "we go to the bargaining table and management asks, 'Don't you ever get tired of asking for more and more?' The answer is, as long as science and technology through the creation of abundance makes more not only economically just, but makes more and more econmically necessary—the answer is yes, we are going in year after year and ask for more and more because we are entitled to more and more and more."

When someone mentioned the distant future, Walter said, "The possibilities of human progress are as unlimited as the creative genius of the free human spirit," he said. "We are now approaching the point where man becomes less an economic being and more a cultural being. In the future, it's possible that the average worker will spend less time making Fords, and more time working on a concerto or a painting or scientific research."

Hard-boiled newspapermen stared agog at this vision of factory workers turned artists and composers. Was Reuther really serious? Absolutely, he told them, and he added: "We'll never know how much wasted genius went unborn because of the sheer human task of feeding families." Well, someone asked, a bit sarcastically, when might we expect this golden age of the worker-artist to become reality? Walter grinned his engaging grin. "I don't know," he said. "But it will come much sooner than the National Association of Manufacturers expects."

In such rapier-like flashes of wit, in such far ranging visions, one gets the measure of the man. He always seems a jump ahead of the jibe of the minute or the issue of the decade. A few years ago, a supervisor was showing him through a Ford automated plant that can turn out an engine block, untouched by human hands, in less than 15 minutes. Walter was impressed. He remembered the long hours of hard hand labor that went into the fashioning of each such block during his early days in Detroit. Sensing this, the man from Ford got in a sly dig. "Aren't you worried about how you're going to collect union dues from those machines?"

Quick as a whip came the answer. "Not at all. What worries me is how *you* are going to sell *them* Ford cars."

Only a sharp mind, and one that had probed all angles of such complex issues, could have come up with so swift and devastating a retort. This is undoubtedly the reason that Reuther overawes many persons, even as he scares others. Rabbi Morris Adler, of Detroit, who has served on committees with Walter and observed him in action, has remarked: "Some people never forgive a man with a new idea."

The fear of the new, the fear of change, powerfully sway the wealthy and conservative classes who usually want mainly to preserve the status quo that has done so well by them. To such persons, Walter is a disruptive and menacing influence, and the mere mention of his name is enough to set their teeth on edge.

The reaction, a combination of prejudice and fright and hate, is strengthened by Walter's steadfast, unwavering championship of liberal Democratic interests. His UAW-CIO war chest has bankrolled the Democratic Party in Michigan for years, much to the dismay of industrialists who had fallen into the habit of thinking political parties should be bankrolled only by them. Their ire was not lessened by Reuther's success. He and the labor backing he wields were generally held responsible for the election of seven successive Democratic governors, the most prominent of whom was the repeatedly elected G. Mennen (Soapy) Williams. It was not until 1962 that George Romney, president of American Motors, a man of great charm in his own right, broke the pattern. Walter, who campaigned hard against Romney, throws himself into such political battles with all the fervor with which in the old days he used to plot a sit-down strike or lead a picket line.

The result has been that, while liberals love him, conservatives fear and hate him, and the Republicans, who represent predominantly conservative interests and so become the target of some of his keenest thrusts, seize upon him as a handy whipping boy. "When you have widespread apathy," one highly placed GOP strategist in Washington once confessed, "you need a devil to get the voters aroused. Reuther's a pretty good devil." This cynical exaggeration of the Reuther "menace" serves its partisan political purpose and probably instils enough doubts about Reuther in enough minds to make it highly unlikely he will ever himself run for high political office. But it is significant that it has little effect in areas of society where ideas count—among the great of the world and the world's eager, questioning youth. Reuther's appeal to both classes has been demonstrated many times.

When he spoke at the University of California, for example, he set an attendance record surpassed only once—by Alfred C. Kinsey, talking on his specialty, sex, a subject with which even Walter couldn't quite compete. Among world leaders he has numbered many admirers: Chester Bowles and Eleanor Roosevelt in the United States; Aneurin Bevan and leaders of the British Labour Party in England; Prime Minister Jawaharal Nehru in India. The British Labour leaders, indeed, have been so taken with Reuther that they have hailed him as a man of cabinet stature, and in India, after one whirlwind tour, he became practically a folk hero.

It happened in 1956. The Eisenhower administration, sorely troubled by India's neutralism and dangerous drift toward the Communist camp, needed an unofficial emissary in New Delhi, and they decided to send Walter. It was an excellent choice. He proved worse than a dose of hemlock to the Indian Reds. The local press commented admiringly on his prim, but sturdy, democratic quirks—at receptions he wouldn't wear a dinner jacket—and in his speeches he tan-

Dressed for a village feast on the India tour

gled head on with hecklers and Red debaters, handling them with devastating wit, speaking the heady language of American freedom and idealism, all mixed in with his faith in people and a better future.

His triumph in India was repeated in December 1962, when he toured Japan. Again the Communists protested his presence, picketing, waving signs urging him to go home, heckling. It was opposition that, to Walter, was like a shot of adrenalin. He took on all comers, debating, arguing, convincing. Japanese youth was so impressed with him that, when he left, the New York *Times* commented that observers in Japan agreed he had done more good than any American visitor in ten years.

Such is the man, such the basis of his tremendous appeal to those not hidebound by the thinking of the past or blinded by their own self-interest. He boils down all the problems of our time, of our conflict with Communism, into one fundamental, underlying issue—the greater good of the individual. "Our problem is to make our more complex society better serve the needs of the people, of the individual," he says.

He has nothing but contempt for the rigid type of business mentality that still believes "there is some sacred magic in the words 'free enterprise,' " and that if "government would just get out of the picture and do nothing, everything would magically solve itself and be fine." "Such men are still living in the 18th century," Walter says. "They don't understand the first thing about the world they live in."

As he sees it, the enormous boon of modern technology, of automation, must be made to serve the good, not just of a management-ownership class interested in greater profits, but the welfare of all the people. This means inevitably planning and sharing on a scale never conceived in a pure free enterprise economy. The problem is to make the mass society of the 20th century serve and strengthen individual man, not crush him; this in Walter Reuther's view is the battle that lies at the heart of our ideological struggle with Communism.

"Either they will win or we will," he says, "because their system, or ours, is best able to meet the needs and better the life of the individual. If we cannot win the battle on those terms, then we don't deserve to win it.

"I'm convinced that we can win it, that we can do far better then the Communists can ever do—if we once realize what it is all about. Our job is not to make people conform, but to promote the greatest possible amount of individual freedom and discussion, on which depends the greatest amount of human creativity. Our problem is to use all the resources and potentialities of our huge, complex technological system—and to use them to promote the greatest degree of individual well-being, liberty, and creativity. There is no limit to what we can accomplish once we see the issue in those terms."

And there is no limit to Walter Reuther's vision of the future once that issue is understood. He is a man who, in his faith in the resources of people, looks towards a limitless horizon.